ACTIVE DUTY ENTREPRENEURSHIP

For God, Country, and the New American Dream

MALCOLM ALLEN

Fables of the Active Duty Entrepreneur

Copyright © 2019 by **Malcolm Allen**

All rights reserved. No part of this book may be reproduced or transmitted in any form or by any means without written permission of the author.

Web: www.Unconditional.org
ISBN: 9781072374817

Acknowledgments

To all the active duty military personnel and their spouses around the world; thank you for your service.

CONTENTS

Introduction: A Man Named Joe 1

The Day Will Come: Who Are the Veteran Entrepreneurs? 13

The Veteran Entrepreneur's Chance: Turning Disasters into Opportunities...34

Do Today's Veterans Have an Entrepreneurship Gap? (Answer: Not Yet) 56

It's Never Too Soon: Active Duty Entrepreneurship...77

When Women Take Charge: Today's Veteran Women and Entrepreneurship 102

Married to the Military: Military Spouses and Entrepreneurship 118

Why Veteran Start-ups Help Us All: America's Best Business Owner...133

Veterans in Crisis: When the Going Gets Tough........145

About the Author..156

Introduction: A Man Named Joe

People who met him seemed to automatically think of him as a kind of "universal soldier," but to the others in his platoon he was just plain "Joe." Joe hated the smell of this place as much as any of the other guys. Ever since he and his unit had landed in the country, the odor had followed them, permeating their clothes and settling into their skin. This stench, combining burning oil, piles of feces, and worse, made every day a little harder, fraying tempers, draining energy, and giving every soldier one more reason to yearn for home. When Joe had first arrived, he'd thought that it smelled like death, but he'd worked hard to cast that notion out of his head. Death was close enough . . . no reason to dwell on it. Nonetheless, the odor was always there, searing his nostrils as he went to sleep each night, and reminding him of the nightmare that was this place as soon as he woke up each morning.

Joe had been there for almost a year, and he'd seen more horrors than he'd imagined were possible. When he'd first arrived, he'd meant to start a journal, but the thought had faded. There was no need to keep a record. He knew that when he finally returned home, he would remember many more details than he wanted to.

Joe had seen streets strewn with dead, wounded, and stray body parts. He'd watched small children scurrying away from approaching soldiers after stripping fresh corpses of their valuables. He'd lost buddies to bullets, IEDs, and one had been sent back home after a young boy had knifed him. Through it all, Joe had witnessed the daily efforts of people trying to rebuild their lives, homes, and families despite the continuing destruction all around them.

He was looking at evidence of that destruction right now. They'd come out to this neighborhood expecting trouble. During the previous month's bombing, the area had been shelled mercilessly. Direct hits had demolished two buildings, and none of the neighborhood's structures had escaped damage. All the residents had fled. For a time, the surviving buildings had stood empty, but then a couple of enemy snipers had noticed one house with potential. The structure had a set of upper-story windows, and a roof above, and both offered a perfect view of the road about a hundred yards beyond. One of their bullets had killed an American soldier the day before. Other Americans had pursued the snipers, but they had disappeared down the empty streets.

Joe and his unit had come out to pacify the area. When they arrived, the buildings and streets were hot, dusty, and empty. Though the stench was as strong as ever, there were no bodies, and the residents had left nothing of value behind. The Americans had searched for two hours but hadn't found a soul. In their search of the area buildings, they found the main sniper nest on the roof. A heap of spent shell casings told the tale. Now two of Joe's men were preparing a set of explosives to demolish the building.

"Looks like the building was some kind of store," said a voice from behind Joe. He looked around and saw it was Corporal Barnes.

"How so?" Joe asked.

"A whole lot of bagged bread—old, and hard as rocks, probably abandoned a long time ago, when the bombs started dropping. Also, there's an empty cash box, and the kinds of bins and shelves we might see in a convenience store at home, but a whole lot dirtier. The upstairs area looked like it was home for the owners. They left, and I guess they never came back."

Joe wiped sweat from his face and shook his head. "That's sad. They lost their business. I grew up in a place just like that. Mom and Dad started a corner grocery just before I was born, and we lived upstairs. We all worked in there until they sold it."

"Did they get a lot for it?" Barnes asked.

Joe shrugged. "They got enough to pay off the mortgage and supplement their social security checks, but that's about all. Still, that store gave us a special place in the neighborhood. It still does, because people remember it." He looked at the building that was about to be blown up and shook his head. "The things we have to do . . . "

"Yeah, but would you rather catch a bullet out there on the road?" Barnes asked.

"Oh, I know we have to do it," Joe answered, "and I know why we have to do it. I don't want to catch that bullet any more than you do. But I also know all the work they must've put into their store. What are they going to do when they come back, and find their whole building is just short of being rubble?"

"Do you really think anybody's going to come back here?"

"Maybe not, but in a way that's even worse. You know, those are the kind of folks we should be cultivating: small business owners—the ones who are willing to take risks. They built what was here before, and now we should be helping them rebuild bigger and better . . . though maybe it shouldn't overlook the road."

"Do you think it's worth it?" the corporal asked.

"Yeah, I do," said Joe. "A store like that is an essential piece of any neighborhood. You've gone through the other buildings. Were any of them laid out like this store?"

"No," Barnes said. "They're all homes."

"Then this was almost certainly their hub. Besides providing necessities, a corner store is a place where people meet, talk, and plan their days. If instead of destroying it, we could help somebody reopen it, that would truly be a ray of hope around here."

Barnes nodded, but then shook his head, saying: "We got to blow it up. You know that."

"You're right," Joe admitted, "but eventually people will start moving back here, and when they do, they're going to need a store like that one. As I get closer to going home, I think about that stuff more and more. When I get back to civilian life, I want to start a business."

"What kind of business?" Barnes asked.

"Store . . . shop . . . service . . . I'm not sure," Joe replied. "I want to make some money; I want to provide jobs; I want to help people find the things they need. But while we've been here, I've learned that there's something else: A truly successful business is all about connecting people with hope. I never thought about that until I came here, but it's true."

"Did your parents' store do that?"

Joe nodded. "They hoped to make enough to raise my sister and me. They hoped to pay off the mortgage and have something for their old age. They hoped they could add something to the neighborhood—be good citizens. They wanted the neighborhood to be safe, and healthy for us kids. The other people in the neighborhood hoped they could do things like that, too. That's a part of why they came to our store every day. People supported each other's businesses. It made sense."

"When you open your business, will you be doing it in your old neighborhood?" Barnes asked.

"I don't know," Joe replied. "I could open a store serving the neighborhood or figure out a service I could offer worldwide."

"Worldwide? You do have hope, don't you?"

"Sure, I do." Joe nodded toward the building where soldiers were already placing explosives. "If we're going to destroy the past, we have to be ready to build a future."

Barnes looked at him thoughtfully. "When we get home, let's keep in touch. I might be asking you for a job."

* * *

Joe and Corporal Barnes are hardly unique in the U.S. military. Their conversation could happen in any of the far-flung outposts of American power scattered across the globe. Most people serving in the military think a lot about what they will do when they get out. Many soldiers use their time in the service to get useful job training they can profit from when they return to civilian life. Some learn the basics of responsibility, punctuality, and cooperation with others. Many service members pick up basic workplace skills. Others receive a formal education, earning certifications, diplomas, and degrees.

A lot of returning soldiers will use their new training to find jobs in manufacturing, construction, government, or various other sectors of our economy.

Some prefer working for a good company and taking direction from the top. Others go back to school to learn new trades or professions. Many veterans end up as teachers in our schools, helping students develop untapped talents.

Finally, there are the ones like Joe. After joining the military to see the world, soldiers like Joe start at the bottom as lowly privates. Starting in boot camp, they learn the benefits of discipline and organization. As they advance through the enlisted ranks, they gain a sharp appreciation of teamwork, and what it can accomplish. By the time they reach the ends of their hitches, most of them have developed values that promote endurance, cooperation, and constructive thinking.

This is the point where their parents and grandparents thought about buying homes. To them, a house was the key to security. Quite a few of today's veterans recognize that they live in an increasingly fast-paced world. They want homes, but they also want to start businesses and push them to their full potential. Like so many others exiting the military, these soldiers no longer want to spend their days following someone else's orders. They want to build things, create systems, and make profits—all while making the world a better place.

Though the military relies on obedience and acceptance of authority, it also encourages individual initiative and intelligent innovation. In many ways, it is a breeding ground for future entrepreneurs. The American military has always been home to entrepreneurship, from revolutionary times onward. While George Washington was leading the nation's first army, he was also running a farm. The same was true of General Jackson in the War of 1812. Both men returned to their farmwork after the fighting was done. Among those who served in the Civil War were tens of thousands of small business owners. The World Wars of the last century made our permanent military bigger than it had ever been. Its members began receiving training in transportation, communication, logistics, and even health care—skills in areas that would be useful in the civilian world.

It's never too early for a service member to begin the move to entrepreneurship. A future entrepreneur might even be able to start his or her business while still on active duty. Whether the soldier needs it then or later, the military remains one of the best places to get excellent training for the business world.

Joe looked at a battleground and saw the potential for peace, prosperity, and profit. As he did that, he was following one of the American military's oldest, most useful traditions: that of building hope where there was none.

THE DAY WILL COME: WHO ARE THE VETERAN ENTREPRENEURS?

Our story about Joe is a composite of real people, places, and situations. If you are serving in America's military, you know a lot of men and women living out similar stories. Throughout the world, America's military is known not only for its awesome power, but also for the compassion, decency, and initiative displayed by its members. Though we might inspire fear with our weapons and firepower, when the shooting has stopped, our soldiers still carry the most potent weapon in the American arsenal: real hope for peace and freedom.

When a young person is discharged from the military, he or she doesn't leave those qualities behind. They are still present, sharpened by experience, and ready for use in the civilian world. If you use all the skills, tools, and experiences that you gained in the military, you will have a huge advantage as you reenter civilian life.

According to a 2017 report from the Small Business Association on veteran-owned businesses, veterans own the majority share in over two-and-a-half million companies in the United States. Almost all of these were classified as "small businesses." Half were based out of the ex-vets' homes.

Many of these businesses are part-time ventures run by stay-at-home spouses or freelance companies whose owners hope to expand them into full-time occupations. That's reflected in a 2017 Census Bureau study, which measured the percentage of veteran-owned businesses with no employees, finding that they were 82.5% of these start-ups. Most veterans who are starting businesses want to expand enough to hire employees. According to the Census study, the 442,000 vet-owned businesses that do hire employ over five million people. One of these employers is Army veteran and military spouse, Sarah Stahl (a real individual, not a composite, as will be true of everyone mentioned, unless otherwise noted).

Sarah was still in high school when she felt the first stirrings of entrepreneurial ambition. She was always good at starting projects and leading others through the power of inspiration. Her marks were better than average, but she didn't feel that she would ever thrive in the classroom. Though she did not think college was the right road for her, she did want to keep learning and growing. The military looked like a great option. It was a place where she could get training in skills that would still have value in civilian life, and it allowed her to see the world.

Stahl served three years, training, and then working as a finance specialist. While she was still on active duty, she met her future husband, Daniel. In seventeen years of marriage, they have had three children. Sarah has spent the last fourteen years of that as a military spouse. Daniel was a lifer and retired three years ago, and the family has been making a successful transition to civilian life.

When Sarah left the military, her goals were to raise her children and explore the world of small business. Reviving the entrepreneurial spirit she'd felt in high school, Sarah went where her skills and talents led her. She'd always had a knack for arts and crafts, so she began designing and selling wedding invitations on Etsy. Having an online business allowed Sarah to work from anywhere. That gave her the freedom to stay at home with her children when they were still young.

Sarah's entrepreneurship has been a difficult but ultimately rewarding experience. Like all entrepreneurs, one of her first concerns was financing. "I looked into getting a start-up business loan, but I'm nervous about funding and interest rates," she told an interviewer. "I've been bootstrapping the business, using whatever cash I have on hand. I was looking for funding for a solid brick-and-mortar, but the debt scares me. I do want to invest in the business and keep growing, but I'm not sure if I should go to an investor or get funding. There are still a lot of decisions to be made."

A brief encounter through her website led Sarah to her future business partner: Merrilee Hale. "I had an unusual request for a World of Warcraft wedding invitation . . . I asked on an Etsy forum for anyone who could help, and Merrilee answered." After working on several jobs together, the two began a partnership online. They felt comfortable making this alliance even though they had never met. Working together online every day made them feel as close as sisters. The name of the company they built is Avant Creative.

The biggest obstacle arose unexpectedly in 2017. Early that autumn Sarah and Merrilee met for the first time. That went well, but barely a month later Merrilee died suddenly, and the tragedy nearly wrecked the fledgling business. The women had taken on two partners, but as Sarah later told an interviewer: "[Merrilee] knew the other two partners better. Out of necessity, we've had to band together to get a hold of things. We've had to go through this crisis together, so we're moving towards a partnership."

Avant Creative weathered that tragic crisis, and with Sarah providing much of the leadership, today the company is thriving. Sarah is on social media every day, promoting her business. She also regularly hosts "Reinventing Marketing" on Facebook. She does this in real time, listening to concerns, answering questions, and sharing her experience and wisdom. She has also established a robust presence on the business-oriented social media platform, LinkedIn. In her work on that site and others, she is creating a brand to attract more entrepreneurs like herself.

When asked about the hardest thing she's faced in the business world, Sarah cites "the fact that there isn't anyone to fall back on. I constantly feel like I'm out on a limb, recreating the wheel." When asked about the benefits, she's quick to say: "My schedule. My husband and I have three kids, and it's invaluable to be able to adjust my work schedule; however, I need to in order to both support and be available for our children."

Sarah had the advantages of a supportive family and being intensely goal-oriented. Not all returning vets have those benefits. Some vets have a hard time adjusting to the looser structure of civilian life. These former soldiers have a lot to figure out before they can make any decisions about entrepreneurship. When FOX NFL insider Jay Glazer became aware of the problems returning vets face, he teamed with U.S. Army Special Forces veteran, and former Seattle Seahawk, Nate Boyer. Together these athletes founded Merging Vets and Players. This organization matches recently separated combat veterans and former professional athletes. The athletes help vets as they part with their old team—the U.S. military—and find new teams in the civilian world. Many of the veterans become entrepreneurs, starting their own "teams" as they venture into the marketplace.

Boyer sees striking parallels between the world of the NFL and that of the military. "[W]ar fighters and football players need something to fight for once the uniform comes off," Boyer says. "Without a real purpose for the man on your right and left, it can be easy to feel lost."

Glazer and Boyer's organization provides peer support by initiating and fostering these connections between athletes and veterans. In various locations around the country, they offer these team-oriented prospects appropriate physical training and challenges that prepare them for new and different jobs. It's something like an athletic training camp for the business world.

Efforts like those of Glazer and Boyer are crucial for soldiers who are leaving the military. Nearly two hundred thousand sailors, soldiers, and guardsmen reenter civilian life every year. Many have no idea of what they are going to do next and fear an uncertain future. Many won't be prepared. Some veterans find their reentry to civilian life complicated by a residue of service-related problems. Those who have been in conflict zones are often still dealing with their physical and mental wounds. Some find the transition to the more free-form life of a civilian to be full of temptations and pitfalls. For others, the change is complicated by unforeseen events.

Patrick Mudge thought his transition from active duty to civilian status was going smoothly, but then he started hearing of the deaths of some of his friends and commanding officers who were still overseas. Suddenly he felt as if a weight had been put on his shoulders. As Mudge puts it: "I wore the burden deep in my soul." He had started his civilian life as a

Department of Defense contractor in security and protection, but as the years passed inner conflicts ate at him. Unable to let go of his grief, Mudge went through two messy divorces and several career changes. His mind was teetering on the brink when he finally had to admit something was wrong. "[It] took several mentors to come into my life and help me identify who I am and what my values are," he now says. "This was a very humbling process and painful all at the same time. But in the end, I understood who I was and what I believed in."

Mudge took that hard-earned self-knowledge and put it to work in an entirely new field. In Lake Jackson, Texas, he started Tango 1 Services LLC, a pressure washing service that hires disabled veterans. Once it was successful, Mudge used the experience to become an independent consultant helping other new businesses reach success. He's always on the lookout for veteran entrepreneurs. In this role, Mudge is sometimes a motivational speaker at galas, benefits, and other gatherings. When an interviewer recently asked him for his most essential advice to vets, he said: "Focus on positivity and remove toxic people and influences from your daily routine."

Mudge's transition took years, beginning with his departure from active duty. He couldn't create a new and happy life in the present until he'd let go of the past. Sometimes the future overlaps with the present, and entrepreneurial opportunities arrive before the soldier leaves the military. That's what happened to Matthew "Griff" Griffen. In five years as an Army Ranger in Iraq and Afghanistan, Griff saw deep-rooted poverty that seemed resistant to any kind of intervention. Like our example of Joe in the Introduction, Griff truly wanted to help.

Each day he did his job, and after a while, he noticed that some of the people who were making the most difference were entrepreneurs. These people saw that to get ahead as individuals; they had to change their communities. They wanted to give people jobs doing valuable work. Griff watched this, always wondering if he could do something similar. Then one day, in a Kabul shop, he happened to see a boot sole with a flip flop thong for sale. Once he had wrapped his head around that, he got an idea: Combat Flip Flops.

That's his company's name today, but it's a lot more than fun footwear. Griff decided to start a business dedicated to connecting people who want to manufacture unique, but inexpensive items with the people who want to buy them. Impoverished people living in dangerous parts of the world would get to go to work each day, and manufacture items like those Combat Flip Flops for which Western consumers are willing to pay top dollar. A consumer gets cool footwear, a worker gets a comparatively hefty paycheck, and Griff makes a small profit on every sale. He gives enough of that back to make a real difference. According to a recent article: "Every [Combat Flip Flop] product sold puts an Afghan girl in school for a day." Griff even made a recent appearance on Shark Tank—a good sign for any new business.

When Marine Corps Sergeant Matt Demaio was deployed to Mozambique in 2010, he'd heard enough from other infantrymen to know that when he went out on missions, he shouldn't rely on MREs (Meals Ready to Eat), the Army's standard food rations. To supplement, and sometimes replace these, he carried an assortment of protein and nutrition bars. Sometimes he needed quick energy, and other times, he needed something that could substitute for a real meal. He had bars for each of these purposes, as well as other bars for other specific needs.

Carrying all those different nutrition bars could get crazy. Demaio always had to consider the tasks he had ahead of him before deciding whether he wanted protein, or sugar, or maybe vitamin-packed carbs. Soon he imagined a new kind of nutrition bar—one that had enough of everything a working soldier might need.

By 2011 Demaio had become a civilian again, and he was living just outside New York City on Long Island. He was a full-time student who was also working an almost full-time job, but in his occasional idle moments, he still recalled his idea for a better nutrition bar. He couldn't stop thinking about it, and within a year after being discharged from the Army, he was experimenting with recipes in his kitchen.

In the beginning, Matt just made bars for Army friends who were still serving in Afghanistan, but by the time he earned his first college degree, he saw signs that this could be more. His friends thought the bars really worked. They were always asking for more and offering to pay him. That's when the idea occurred to him that he could use the products of his experiments to start his first small business. "The feedback I got from my buddies . . . was, 'This is great. It keeps me full, and it keeps me going,'" Demaio told an interviewer. "That's when it clicked."

Demaio wasn't in a hurry. Three more years passed before he made the decision to found Condition One Nutrition. At first, he kept his day job and only worked on his new venture during off- hours, but soon he was putting in forty hours per week on his nutrition bars, and they were beginning to sell.

When he started his business, Demaio had only his income from his day job, credit cards, and the proceeds from cashing out his 401k. He never looked for bank loans or investors, and none approached him. He did find mentors, and they helped. Finally, in December 2017, Matt gave a presentation at one of the quarterly forums of the Long Island Capital Alliance, a group that hooks up aspiring entrepreneurs with angel investors. After closing a financing deal, Matt felt optimistic. "I'm in discussions for additional funding from other angel investors I met through LICA," he told a local reporter. He declined to discuss how much funding he'd received, but he told the reporter he intends to use it as working capital covering marketing and sales costs.

There are always some vets who come home involuntarily due to injury or illness, and this is often followed by discharge. When Chris Kowalik returned from the Middle East as a Service- Disabled veteran, she was thrust into an unexpected transition to civilian life. She had aimed to make her career in the Marines, but she also had a deep understanding of the military mantra: "No plan survives the first contact." A resourceful Marine, Chris vowed to find another way to serve her country. This led her to start a company called ProFeds, a service that helps federal employees plan for healthy, happy retirements.

When she was still on active duty overseas, Chris was an Arabic Linguist and Signals Intelligence Analyst. Her work helped military units translate radio signals so that U.S. land, air, and sea forces could coordinate their operations more effectively. Simplifying military communications helped American commanders create streamlined strategies that were flexible enough to adapt to evolving circumstances. Her translations were key tools in this military planning and execution.

In her civilian business, Chris does a different kind of translating. Instead of converting Arabic to English, she translates the confusing numbers and formulas of personal finance into plain English. She does this for federal workers throughout the country, helping them identify the tools they need to create solid, secure retirement plans.

"Getting here was not easy," Chris told a recent interviewer. "I channeled my military mindset along with the sheer grit and tenacity that comes with being a U.S. Marine, to power through the tough landscape of entrepreneurship. The hard work has certainly paid off. I'm thrilled to be celebrating my tenth year in business this year."

These transitions and the problems that come with them are nothing new. Even in ancient times, soldiers often faced rocky transitions from wartime conditions to peacetime activities. Three thousand years ago, the ancient Greeks told dramatic stories of the crises soldiers faced after they had returned from the Trojan wars. In the last century, finding solutions for the problems of returning vets was a major issue after both World Wars, Korea, and Vietnam. Hollywood made movies about it, and Washington addressed the problem with the passage of the Servicemen's Readjustment Act, otherwise known as the GI Bill. This World War II measure provided veterans with health care, education, job training, and housing—just what returning soldiers wanted. Though the law did not specifically emphasize entrepreneurship, it did provide vets with low-interest loans for education, training, a home, or small business investment.

Many enterprising vets of that era avoided bank loans. Instead, they used the law's benefits to support themselves while they were starting businesses. Prior to the GI Bill, most veteran benefits had been health-related or severely limited cash payouts, but now these benefits were codified, organized, and many of the benefit programs were designed to be permanent. One of the new law's temporary provisions gave each vet $20 per week for up to a year as he looked for a new job (close to $300 per week in today's dollars). A special fund was created to pay out this money, and many vets applied. Those who did were called the "52/20 Club." Opponents of this fund predicted that most returning vets would take every cent they could and that it would run dry before the end of the first year. They could not have been more wrong. Most of those who joined the 52/20 Club were only in it for a few months, or even weeks. These men were eager to start families, and they wanted to work. They found jobs quickly, and by the end of the year, barely a fifth of the fund had been spent.

The creators of the 52/20 fund had imagined most veterans would use the money to support themselves until they found jobs in factories, stores, offices, and on construction sites, but many of the recipients avoided these traditional jobs. Instead, they used the government checks to support themselves while pouring their time, and any extra cash, into their fledgling businesses. One astounding fact about the returning soldiers from World War II was that over half of them started small businesses. Veterans of the conflicts in Korea and Vietnam were almost as enterprising, with over a third beginning a business within a few years of coming home.

One of these veterans was martial arts legend, Chuck Norris. When he joined the military one of Norris's chief motivations was to put some muscles on his then-thin frame. Stationed for three years in Korea in the late 1950s, Norris earned a black belt in karate and a brown belt in judo. To this day Norris credits his training in these arts with giving him a better outlook on life. As he puts it: "I realized that there was nothing I couldn't achieve if I just had determination and persistence. In gaining the ability to defend myself, I also learned the discipline and self-respect I needed for the rest of my life."

When he got back to the States, Norris worked as a file clerk for Northrop Aviation, but he also began giving lessons in the martial arts. Lessons turned into formal classes, and by 1968, when he was beginning an unprecedented seven-year reign as World Middleweight Karate Champion, Norris opened the first of what would soon be a chain of thirty-two karate schools. Long before he got the big movie roles that made him famous, Norris had already made a fortune as a veteran entrepreneur.

Today's veterans are returning to a nation where many see entrepreneurship as the key to success. More and more Americans are learning to market their skills and ideas, turning them into profit-making products and services. Those who are still in the military often find opportunities for training and education in areas that have real value in the civilian world. Active duty soldiers should take advantage of these and prepare themselves to start and lead new enterprises. When the time comes to exchange military discipline for the freedoms and responsibilities of civilian life, a veteran should be prepared to take the initiative.

THE VETERAN ENTREPRENEUR'S CHANCE: TURNING DISASTERS INTO OPPORTUNITIES

When most civilians think of our military; they picture soldiers, sailors, and pilots deployed to trouble spots throughout the world. On TV they see uniformed Americans in deserts, jungles, mountains, and on the high seas. Americans who live near military bases see off–duty soldiers in their stores and businesses every day. But occasionally a civilian crisis calls their soldiers from their bases, and these young Americans enter our communities for missions of prevention, rescue, and restoration. They are usually responding to out-of-control problems, and they are usually a big part of the solution. That's what happened in Flint, Michigan, in 2016.

In early 2013 Ed Kurtz, the state-appointed city manager of Flint, announced a switch to a new source for the city's water. The financially challenged city had been considering a change for years, and now the crisis team that had been put in charge of the city's government felt the time had come. Flint residences and businesses would stop receiving water from their then-supplier, the Detroit Water and Sewage Authority, and the city would begin work on a long-range plan to dig tunnels to Lake Huron to tap its waters. This operation would take several years, so in the interim, they would get their water from the Flint River that ran directly through the town. For decades the river had been used only as a backup source.

This created a situation where an increasing percentage of Flint's daily water supply had to pass through the oldest piping in the city even after the water had undergone filtration. Some of this piping was in the form of lead lines built over a century ago for Flint's first public water system. This created new problems, and by the end of the year, residents and businesses were seeing and tasting those problems in the water coming out of their taps. Lead levels were skyrocketing, and the local General Motors plant reported corrosion in its car parts due to water contaminants. GM was the first corporation to complain to city officials, formally asking that Flint switch back to Detroit water in October of 2013.

In 2014 the employees of Flint's public library began noticing discoloration and a bad taste in their tap water. City officials assured them that the water was fine, but the library's dubious employees made their own switch to bottled water. Since then, Flint's public library has become a vocal proponent of change in Flint's water system, and they have also made themselves into a conduit for free bottled water for the entire community.

In 2015 Flint made a deal to bring back Detroit water, while commissioning several studies aimed at reaching a fuller understanding of the crisis. Unfortunately, the Flint system was still suffering the effects of Flint River water and the city's aging infrastructure. In September of that year, water quality expert, Dr. Marc Edwards, led a team from Virginia Tech as they tested lead levels throughout the area. By the following January, they were reporting that the "very corrosive" Flint water was "causing lead contamination in homes." The levels of contamination were startling. Edwards's team detected some lead levels as high as 13,200 parts per billion (ppb). Safe levels are below fifteen ppb.

The Virginia Tech report came in early January of 2016. By January fifteenth, Michigan's governor, Rick Snyder, had asked for help from the Federal Emergency Management Agency (FEMA), and at the same time, he activated units in Michigan's National Guard. The Guardsmen were assigned to help

American Red Cross workers distribute water filters to affected homes and businesses. Within a week, two hundred soldiers were knocking on doors in Flint, and helping residents find convenient sources for good, clean water.

As the crisis worsened, it became a national story. When Major George Hurd of the Texas National Guard learned about it, he decided to deploy to Flint on his own. He and other Guard members loaded Hurd's truck with well over a thousand bottles of water and other necessities. Hurd and his fifteen-year-old daughter, Olivia, then drove all the way to Michigan. There they worked with local agencies and churches to identify the neediest recipients. "Part of it comes from my experience overseas in Egypt, Iraq, and Afghanistan, where we gave out bottled water to children all across that region," Hurd told a reporter. "When I sat back . . . seeing the disaster [in Flint], I just thought there wasn't enough attention. It affected me to the core, and instead of just complaining about it, I decided to do something about it."

As we've noted, we often forget that our soldiers don't just fight wars. Sometimes their battles are with disasters here at home, both man-made and natural. In Flint, two hundred soldiers worked tirelessly to help parents protect kids from lead poisoning and to save a town from the effects of its potentially fatal choices. As these soldiers complete their mission, some have thoughts about other ways to help similar victims. Some of our soldiers overseas are assisting residents in the creation of entirely new systems for water, sewage, health, transportation, and education. The skills they are developing can be put to creative and entrepreneurial uses back home. Cities like Flint need help from water experts before they find themselves in a crisis. Guardsmen like Hurd know this problem well. Too often, the crises they face would have been avoidable if just a few simple precautions had been in place.

That's often true of disasters, both man-made and natural. In 2018, California and other western states faced the worst set of wildfires in the region's history. The biggest was named: The Camp Fire. It started in Butte County on the morning of November eighth, then roared across about twenty-five square miles of urban sprawl and forest, damaging or destroying over fourteen thousand homes. It was the state's deadliest fire on record, killing eighty-five people.

The Camp Fire came in a year when California experienced seven huge conflagrations that now have a place on the list of the state's twenty most destructive fires in history. The Camp Fire came just as area residents were marking the first anniversary of California's next-most-destructive fire event, the Tubbs Fire, which was centered near the wine-country town of Santa Rosa. That one destroyed fifty-five hundred structures and claimed twenty-two victims.

In fast-moving disasters like fires, the military usually can't do much actual firefighting. Instead, their efforts are often aimed at supporting emergency systems in the disaster's aftermath. That was the case with California's Camp Fire. Several days after the fire started, when a National Guard contingent of one hundred military police arrived on the scene, they weren't there to actively put out fires. Instead, these guardsmen and their service dogs were trained to locate and identify human remains. They were entering a town in the Sierra foothills with a population of about twenty-seven thousand residents. Many of us learned about this tragic site, along with its ironic name, when we were watching the news: Paradise, California. It had been an affluent community where happy residents were living the American Dream. Now it was nothing but rocks and mud. Sadly, the guardsmen and their dogs found quite a few bodies among the ruins.

Over forty million people live in California. Most of them aren't going anywhere, but neither is the threat of fire. Fires threaten every new development, and each new suburban house is like an open invitation for sparks. "I think of fire as a driverless car," says Arizona State University fire researcher Stephen Pyne. "It's just barreling down the road integrating everything around it. It's a reaction—it takes its character from its context." This sounds a lot like what happens in war.

Many people feel that controlling, stopping, and cleaning up after these fires is a job for various government agencies. In most ways, this is true, but the government can't do everything. At some point, private citizens must take the initiative to prevent as many fires as possible and to rebuild their communities in ways that inhibit or prevent fires. Hundreds of tasks grow out of these efforts, including rebuilding structures and recasting landscapes, so they are more resistant to fires. Some guardsmen see this better future rising from the ashes left by tragedy. Some of the smart, enterprising soldiers will go back to civilian life and apply their knowledge and experience to the problems of fireproofing and fire prevention. They will act as entrepreneurs in the private sphere. Their innovations will change our communities, making all of us safer.

One of the things these firefighters notice is the limited effect of fire codes. Though California and its jurisdictions are making codes more and more strict, they don't often have enough personnel to enforce the new regulations. "[E]nforcement falls on the local municipal agencies and fire departments," says Crystal Kolden, a fire scientist at the University of Idaho, "and often times they simply don't have the resources." This problem starts inside individual homes and businesses. In its enforcement of building codes, the government plays an important role in encouraging property owners to make their structures safer, but private contractors usually do the actual work.

As wildfires threaten more and more areas, soldiers will play a bigger role in rescue and recovery operations. Among them are future entrepreneurs who will start businesses in these devastated regions, or back in their own hometowns. These vets will help communities rise from the ashes and will help owners of homes and businesses prevent the worst effects of the next fire.

Soldiers might find similar opportunities to use their enterprise and initiative when helping communities recover from the opposite of fire: rain and windstorms. When the worst storms are raging, and first responders are swamped, that's when America needs its military here at home. Texans learned that during Hurricane Harvey two years ago.

Harvey was a long, slow-moving storm whose center skirted the shoreline of the Gulf of Mexico. It made landfall five times, three in Texas, and two in Louisiana. When it first hit land, Harvey was a Category 4 storm, with winds of 140 miles per hour, but most of the problems were caused by the forty inches of rain accompanying the storm. Army personnel, ground vehicles, and helicopters proved vital in initial efforts to rescue people, but repairs and rebuilding didn't happen until after they were gone. These later efforts required many hours from thousands of workers. Some were paid from public funds, but owners of homes and businesses were looking for skilled workers who could help them rebuild in ways that would shield them from the worst effects of the next storm. This was a prime opportunity for soldier-entrepreneurs. They had seen the storm itself and knew firsthand what these property owners were up against.

Harvey caused more damage in dollars than any other hurricane in history except Katrina, with which it is tied. Both storms left price tags of $125 billion in their wakes. Any entrepreneur should understand the full meaning of that number. If states, businesses, and individuals have lost $125 billion worth of property, then at least that much will be spent in the rebuilding effort. In fact, replacing homes and businesses often costs more. New structures will have more frills and new features, and rebuilding is always an opportunity for modernization. All of this—replacement, renovation, and expansion—involves countless tasks, repairing everything from giant warehouses to a homeowner's shed crushed by a falling tree. A school might lose books, desks, or other educational hardware. A marina owner won't be surprised if his docks are damaged and whatever boats were left have been destroyed. Eventually, all these things will be replaced, which means someone must be there to replace them. Guardsmen who have served in these areas have the advantage of knowing the damage firsthand. Any entrepreneurs among them will see these problems as opportunities.

As the magnitude of Harvey became clear, Governor Greg Abbott called the entire Texas National Guard to active duty. Soon, over twelve thousand citizen-soldiers responded. On their arrival in these coastal communities, these guardsmen did everything from piling sandbags around basements to classic rescues of people who had been forced upon their roofs by rising waters. The Guard's quick response in Texas and Louisiana was one of the reasons Harvey's death toll was less than a tenth of that of Katrina.

More and more military training is aimed at disaster relief. Inevitably this overlaps with the local citizens' initial efforts to repair and rebuild their communities. This puts soldiers in a unique position to understand the needs of a community. As Army Colonel Robert Carruthers puts it: "Not a lot of people appreciate or understand that the National Guard also has this homeland defense and response mission in which we respond to natural disasters or terrorist events. That is equally important to the war-fighting, but to those at home, this mission may be more important than the overseas mission."

Carruthers was in a unique position to understand this. The previous October he and his men had helped the residents of Beaver Dam Lake, not far from Columbia, South Carolina, shore up a failing dam.

Their successful efforts had averted unimaginable disasters.

The storm that brought the dam to its breaking point had doused the area with three months' worth of normal rainfall in a single day. In the aftermath, local resident, Jim Lehman, paddled his kayak out to remove the straw from an opening that had been designed to allow water to pass through the dam. Once he began this task, he saw the futility of it, and as he watched the lake water rise, he realized the twenty-four-foot-high dam was in real trouble.

That morning several agencies put together the manpower and equipment to deal with the crisis. Neighborhood leaders, a local landscaper, a highway contractor, an electric utility, state regulators, and the U.S. Department of Homeland Security were joined by the South Carolina National Guard in a race against water as it rushed down from the hills. Though the dam had passed two safety inspections in the previous four years, this storm was testing it in ways its builders had never foreseen.

Eventually, waters from this storm would break through fifteen of Richland County's dams. Eight had received satisfactory inspections within the past four years, according to DHEC records. On that first morning, it looked as if the one at Beaver Dam Lake would hold. It wasn't until the second morning that residents saw the half-moon-shaped dent at the dam's highest point. It had been created by a sinkhole. That was when residents met and decided to send out calls for help to just about everyone they could think of. One of their calls was to the Richland County Sheriff's Office, and another went to DHEC.

"We were calling anyone we could come up with," Lehman said.

Later that Monday the neighborhood association's landscapers answered the emergency call, hauling in ten one-ton sandbags and piling them in front of the sinkhole. They also dug out a two-foot channel, which allowed them to release more water and control the breach more effectively. Residents just hoped they could stave off the worst until the storm waters subsided and they could begin repairs, but when half of the sandbags vanished down the sinkhole, they knew the water was winning.

More help came from Columbia's fire department, and from South Carolina Electric & Gas (SCE&G). The Fire Department did their best to divert the water rising behind the dam into other streams and gullies. The utility company brought in even more sandbags, as well as pipes and better pumping equipment. Soon much of the machinery was there, but there weren't enough people to put it all to use. Finally, the South Carolina National Guard showed up under the leadership of Colonel Carruthers.

Guardsmen began by helping residents fill and carry sandbags. Some went to the sinkhole, while others shored up weak points in the dam. About a hundred guardsmen rotated at the dam, working through that Tuesday and Wednesday with almost no breaks.

On Tuesday night, guardsmen pushed the last giant sandbag into place. Just as it started settling, the whole wall collapsed. Though water levels were dropping, there were still no guarantees that the weakening dam would hold. In the next twenty-four hours, residents appealed to an even wider variety of agencies for help. A highway construction company answered the call with truckloads of huge rocks that the guardsmen piled around the sinkhole. The Department of Homeland Security sent dam experts to consult with the locals. These experts seemed to know what they were doing, and the locals began to feel as if the crisis might be under control.

Then the rock wall collapsed into the sinkhole.

Lehman later said: "Everything we were trying seemed to be logical. It was discouraging." Facing a construction problem that would normally require weeks or even months of review, everyone acted quickly. Crews, including Guard members, simply took all the rocks they had and started piling them wherever they would do the most good. Carruthers and his troops worked with military discipline, which helped keep civilian efforts on track.

After another hundred tons of rock had been added, the lake water stopped eroding the road and earthen dam, and residents finally had good reason to hope that the dam would survive. They and the guardsmen spent the next few days securing the sinkhole. Eventually, a wall of steel sheets was added around the riser, creating a barricade that was meant to stay in place until homeowners could repair the dam properly.

With rock and steel barricades, Lehman described the situation this way: "Now we have on belt and suspenders."

The work of the guardsmen at Beaver Dam Lake helped save the dam, and after undergoing further repairs, it held through the even greater onslaught of

Hurricane Florence in 2018. More bad storms and record rainfalls happened that same year. Colonel Carruthers said his troops had learned techniques in the Lake crisis that helped when they faced other dam breaches in those later storms.

Often these home-based missions require follow-up work that can only be done by private businesses. Opportunities arise in construction, cleanup, landscaping, health care, and other areas of long-term emergency response. These opportunities should be especially appealing to veterans with the proper skills and experience. Soldiers who are trained for battle are also ready for a crisis. When they meet a powerful enemy, they know that it's their job to stop that enemy. This is true whether the opponent is an army or a river.

In addition, many soldiers in today's armed services are developing new skills. These arise from innovative training aimed specifically at disaster response. Once soldiers have learned these skills, they are ready to become freelancers in the civilian world.

Some will start new businesses, and they are likely to employ other vets. These businesses will include entrepreneurial opportunities in landscaping, marine construction, and transportation.

In April 2018 more than four hundred South Carolina Army National Guard soldiers participated in a Guardian Response exercise, along with over a thousand other soldiers from the National Guard and reserves. In the exercise, the soldiers acted as support teams responding to a mock nuclear event involving a dirty nuclear bomb explosion in a generic city. South Carolina's civilian authorities directed these units.

According to their commander, Michigan's Army National Guardsman Major General Michael Stone, "Most of the members of Task Force are citizen-soldiers, ready to help their neighbors recover and get back to a sense of normalcy as soon as possible." As one might imagine, this is very different from more traditional military duties arising out of combat. Army Sergeant Kyle Everett, a combat medic, agreed that this training was atypical. "I'm used to combatting medic training with my unit," Everett said. "What we are doing here would be training for in-state, so we are treating our own citizens, civilians instead of our battle buddies to our left and right. So, it's a little different from what I'm used to normally."

Nonetheless, Everett's medical skills can soon become an entrepreneurial resource, as can his experience in using those skills in a nonmilitary situation. As a medic, Everett is essentially a first responder. This is a field where entrepreneurship is seeing huge growth. Companies like Responder Corporation of Florida are looking for worthwhile opportunities to back entrepreneurs in a variety of first response areas. In a recent cooperative venture with Verizon, they opened a First Responder Lab in Washington, D.C., and selected five companies to use the facilities for research and development aimed at finding better response methods.

Our military services have always been a resource when disasters strike, using their training to save homes and lives. For today's service members, these domestic duties are often an essential part of their jobs. Active military units can make all the difference in the immediate aftermath of disasters, but individual service members might also discover opportunities to create new businesses that will help revive hard-hit communities.

Malcolm Allen

Do Today's Veterans Have an Entrepreneurship Gap? (Answer: Not Yet)

In 1946 Herman Johns returned to Chicago after three years in Europe. He was one of the millions of veterans coming home after World War II. Before the war, Johns had spent a year working as a forest ranger, and two years patrolling city streets for the Chicago Police Department. Before being drafted in 1942, he had been thinking of quitting the force and starting a private investigation business. In the Army, Johns went where his skills and experience led him, starting as a military policeman, then switching to the Counter Intelligence Corps, a precursor to the technical branches of the CIA. There he learned the dangerous art of deactivating bombs that had failed to detonate. Though he'd never allowed himself to imagine failure when performing those nerve-wracking tasks, as he set foot on American soil again, he felt thankful to have survived.

As soon as Johns left the Army, he joined the 52/20 Club, living on his weekly government allowance while he started his business back in Chicago. He applied for, and got, an Illinois investigations license, sought and found some jobs, and almost immediately realized he was in a different business than the one he'd expected. His first job wasn't investigating anything. Johns' first client was a nightclub owner who wanted the investigator to look after the club's star singer. Most of his work was in keeping the wild man sober and out of jail. This led to his being hired as a bodyguard for other celebrities. At one point he was called on to put together a team to keep order at an outdoor rally that drew over five thousand people.

Soon Johns was forming security teams for concerts, sports events, and other public gatherings. He needed new licenses and certifications, and when he got them, he designed, deployed, and operated security systems for large buildings and an industrial park. Most of his many hires were fellow vets. Within ten years, Johns had two dozen full-time employees, and twice that number working part-time. By 1967 he had sold Johns Security to Pinkerton, Inc., making an after-tax profit of over a half million dollars (about $4 million in today's money). He was barely fifty years old.

Johns was one of the first of the returning World War II vets who began their own businesses. Another was future billionaire Jack Taylor, but in Taylor's first try, luck wasn't with him. He had spent the war in the Navy piloting an F6F Hellcat fighter from the deck of the U.S.S. *Enterprise* in the Pacific. While serving his country, Taylor won two Distinguished Flying Crosses and the Navy Air Medal. Unfortunately, after returning home, his entry into the business world was not immediately as successful. On his arrival back in his hometown of St. Louis, Missouri, Taylor began a delivery service. Like many first-time efforts, it didn't work out. He took on too much work, hired too few employees, and too many packages were late or didn't get there at all. Just as he was getting the kinks out of the system, his funds ran dry. It was the kind of failure that leaves an entrepreneur aching for another chance.

With Taylor, that would take a while. After he'd left deliveries behind, Taylor needed regular income before testing the entrepreneurial waters again. In 1948 he took a job selling cars at a Cadillac dealership, but his dreams of starting a small business had not died. It turned out that he was a great salesman, which brought the commissions that became Taylor's working capital. In 1957 he used this, along with backing from the Cadillac dealer, to create the Executive Leasing Company. Starting with only seven cars, Taylor provided them as loaners to customers who'd brought their Cadillacs into the dealership for repairs covered by the warranty. At first, he was paid by the Cadillac dealer whose customers were glad to have the cars. From that Taylor expanded his services, leasing cars to individuals and businesses. Most of these were long-term rentals—a few days or more.

Taylor's car-leasing operation gained popularity, and by 1961, when he turned his first profit, he had a fleet of a thousand leased cars. Up to then he had resisted entering the cutthroat rental market. "We started out saying: 'We don't rent cars,'" he later told a company historian. But when corporate and individual customers kept asking for short-term rentals, Taylor did what Johns had done in his security business— what any good entrepreneur would do—he adapted. By 1963, Taylor was exploring the potential of individual car rentals. He saw that other companies already had the airport travelers covered, but there was a market for local rentals by-the-day. This neglected market became the basis of what would eventually become the $5 billion fortune Taylor would leave to his heirs.

In 1969 Taylor renamed his fast-growing business for the U.S.S. *Enterprise* aircraft carrier, whose deck he'd taken off from and safely touched down on so many times. His business continued to grow. As of 2019, three years after Taylor's death at the age of ninety-four, Enterprise is the largest privately-owned concern in the greater St. Louis area. With over $19 billion in annual revenue, it employs ninety-three thousand people worldwide.

Perhaps the best known of the World War II class of entrepreneurs was the man who may have been its biggest success story: Sam Walton. Walton opened the first store in the chain that would eventually become Walmart in 1962. Thirty years later, when Walton died, his stores had a total workforce of 380,000 employees and sold almost $50 billion worth of merchandise each year. Since then the company has continued to grow, and today, five of Walton's relatives have inheritances that put them among the world's ten richest individuals.

Johns, Taylor, and Walton are just three of the millions of entrepreneurs who served our country in World War II. Millions? Yes. About half of the soldiers returning from that war started their own businesses. With roughly eleven million returning soldiers, that meant over five million of them became entrepreneurs. No accurate figures are available for their companies' survival rates. Many probably went the way of Jack Taylor's short-lived delivery service, but, as in the case of Taylor, some of these failures were preludes to later success.

Today many observers feel that an entrepreneurial crisis is developing among returning vets. These critics look at the 50% entrepreneurship rate among World War II vets and compare it with today's far more modest picture: 4.5% among all vets who've served in the military since 9/11. A study done by the Ewing Marion Kauffman Foundation found that as recently as

1996, vets owned 12.3% of all new businesses. Eighteen years later, in 2014, that figure was down to 5.6%, and since then it has declined even further.

On first look, these numbers show us that today's veteran-entrepreneur rate is less than a tenth of what it was after World War II (4.5% versus 50%), but first looks can be deceiving. In 1945, America was a very different place from the "America" we know today. Vets returning from World War II came home to a nation that felt as if it had been fighting the war right beside them. In a way, it was true. The war reached into every home and touched every person. Every man between eighteen and forty-five was issued a draft card. If a man didn't go into the military, he was expected to work in wartime industries, or volunteer for war-related duties in his hometown. All Americans mobilized for war, and for the first time, women were accepted into newly created branches of the Navy and the Army. No American could escape this all-encompassing national mobilization. Wartime shortages and restrictions affected their lives in countless ways every day. When the Japanese cut off our rubber supply, drivers learned to live with bald tires, and American consumers had to have ration coupons for everything from metals to meat.

Just as most of the men still here at home had been working in war-related jobs, so had a huge proportion of America's women. Thirty-six percent of American women were working full-time outside the home, more than ever had before. Though our mainland never suffered a serious attack, the threat was real. Blackouts and air-raid drills became common. Movies, radio, newspapers, and books all reflected a wartime mentality. Schools and churches joined in drives for scrap iron and other recyclable war materials. Most people at home had a father, brother, or son in the military. Most of these young men had been drafted, and any draft-age male who wasn't in uniform felt a constant sting of shame.

As the war ended, returning soldiers faced a very different economy than the one they had left. In the decade before Pearl Harbor, most of them had known the seemingly endless unemployment of the Depression. With the passage of a few years, and the war's end, these millions of men were discharged (well over 95% were men), and they flooded the job market. Many of them wondered if they were returning to the poverty they'd known before. They were willing to do almost anything to avoid that.

World War II veterans were coming home to a country where the ones who had stayed behind had been making plenty of money. Wages in those wartime industries had been higher than they'd been even in the boom years before the Depression. With so much cash to spend, and so little time to spend it, these workers' savings accounts had mushroomed. In addition, almost everything they'd been making had been shipped overseas to equip America's armies for victory. All those wartime restrictions had kept a heavy lid on the production of consumer goods and civilian housing. With the war over, and so many bank accounts bursting at the seams, most people wanted to spend their money as fast as they could. This produced an ever-growing demand for everything from rental cars to security teams, which in turn created opportunities for millions of entrepreneurs like the ones we've mentioned.

Like Jack Taylor's initial delivery service start-up, many of these fledgling businesses failed. This is true of most small business start-ups in any era, but the problem was even worse for veterans after World War II. Though the cash-rich economy desperately needed new businesses to provide all the things people had been craving and could now afford, many aspiring vet-entrepreneurs didn't know what they were doing. Jack Taylor had never run a delivery service, and when he started one, his inexperience showed. It would be over a decade before he found his formula for success in the car rental business. Herman Johns knew how to investigate a crime or shadow someone, but when he got his first work as a bodyguard, he had to learn a whole new set of skills. If he hadn't mastered them quickly, his tiny start-up would've gone broke. Another vet who had repaired radio equipment for the Navy tried to set himself up as a TV repairman, and quickly found out he couldn't fix most TVs. He went bankrupt. After finally learning the right skills, by 1960 he had his own TV repair business with three employees.

Today's veterans are returning from smaller, less decisive wars. Most of us go through our days without giving too much thought to the various conflicts involving America's military forces. On too many nights we watch the TV news and don't even see a story on our soldiers overseas. When a story does air, it's usually about a battle, bombing, or shoot-out. We seldom see our forces doing the day-to-day work of rebuilding shattered societies. We don't find this in news reports, and what we don't see, we don't think about. Though Americans respect and honor our military, our Armed Forces are not as big or visible as they were in World War II.

Another difference is that the veterans of today's wars return to an economy that's essentially the same as the one they left behind. A veteran who's discharged in 2019 most likely recalls the Great Recession that happened a decade ago, but he's never known an America where tens of millions go to bed hungry every night, or where death from starvation is common. Ours is a booming economy, with plenty of jobs and entrepreneurial opportunities for everyone. Still, we must ask: why don't more of our returning vets take advantage of that to start their own businesses?

If our current vets were starting companies at the same rate as those soldiers who came home after the Korean conflict in the 1950s (our first war after World War II), they would already have 1.4 million start-ups employing almost three million workers. Forty percent of the Korean War vets started businesses after being discharged. According to the Bureau of Labor Statistics, only 4.5% of vets who've served since 9/11 have done that. With a pool of 3.6 million vets, that means about 160,000 of them have begun their own companies. On average, these companies employ two people, so post-9/11 vet-owned start-ups provide about 320,000 jobs, or about one for every nine created by the post–Korean War entrepreneurs.

One of today's most successful veteran entrepreneurs is Joseph Kopser. Kopser was a lifer, spending twenty years in the service before getting out and cofounding the technology start-up, RideScout. After RideScout's initial success, Kopser sold his stake in the company and co-founded GrayLine, a company that helps institutions and businesses manage disruptive change. In this second effort, he has created another success story.

When asked about veteran entrepreneur opportunities then and now, Kopser says: "The differences are so stark it's unbelievable." He feels that one of the biggest reasons for the low numbers of vet entrepreneurs is the lack of in-service mentorship for current military members. He contends that this has produced a situation where far too many vets are content to "get a job and settle" instead of working all the long hours involved in a start-up.

That's a big factor for anyone thinking about a start-up: hours. With many small businesses (especially services conducted online), an entrepreneur might be able to limit hours and control growth. But if you have employees, and an office, store, or any physical headquarters, entrepreneurship will probably require your full-time services, and plenty of overtime as well. That's a part of being the boss. You must decide whether you have the stamina, and are willing to work the hours that are necessary for this kind of entrepreneurial venture.

Another consideration for today's military entrepreneur is that our economy isn't as friendly to new businesses as it was in the 1940s and 1950s. In the '30s, America's economic machine had come to a standstill. Millions were unemployed, and millions more were working only part-time for the lowest wages. War created a boom for large industries, and soon, everyone had a job in a factory or served in the military. This created all those fattened bank accounts, and that money became the financing mechanism for a small business boom like no other. It's no wonder that there were more start-ups after World War II than at any other moment in our history. But they didn't happen all at once. As Sam Walton's 1962 Walmart opening shows, some World War II vets waited decades before making their moves.

In those postwar years, many former NCOs went from commanding platoons to managing assembly lines in factories or being foremen on construction sites. Those were jobs that paid well, allowing vets to build up their savings for later business ventures. That meant many World War II-related entrepreneurial efforts didn't get off the ground until the 1950s, 1960s, or even the 1970s.

In many key areas, today's vets have fewer resources than their predecessors. One thing that's even more difficult is getting a bank loan. Though he would eventually found and succeed with Patriot Commercial Cleaning in St. Louis, Army vet Tim Smith says: "I did approach banks at first, because I didn't have a two-year business history so I couldn't get any financing." After being turned down by banks, Smith finally received a low-interest loan from a vet-friendly nonprofit. "I wouldn't have made payroll without it," he says now.

The recent drop in vet-owned start-ups is a self-perpetuating process. According to one study, vets hire fellow vets 30% more often than non-vets do. With less veteran-owned businesses, fewer veterans are hiring, so fewer are getting hired. Also, those who do find work are less likely to be employed by bosses who are interested in making the most of veterans' skills and abilities, or in understanding their problems. Veterans have so much to give, but many have formed habits tailored to life in wartime environments. Few civilian bosses understand the issues raised by reintegration into civilian life, or the long-term effects of PTSD. Often an impatient boss will only see the obstacles veterans face and won't give any thought to the benefits they bring to the work in the long run. Soldiers are committed to the mission, understand the structure, and are trained to find effective solutions, but many employers won't wait long enough to allow these qualities to emerge.

James Schmeling is an Air Force veteran who, in civilian life, is the executive vice president of the Student Veterans of America, a nonprofit that helps vets find jobs. He notes that many civilians have misperceptions about who vets are. They hear the words "military service," and think of guns, violence, and pain. These people might be sincerely grateful for the protection their soldiers provide, but they won't trust a former soldier with normal peacetimes responsibilities. "There is still some stigma when it comes to employment," Schmeling told an interviewer. "People are afraid to hire vets." This handicap can be added to the lack of financial resources, mentorship, and networking provided to our returning soldiers.

Often overlooked in these comparisons is the element of time. After World War II, millions of vets had experiences like that of Jack Taylor with his delivery service: their first stab at entrepreneurship didn't work out. Nonetheless, they are counted among those five-million-plus postwar start-ups. Many of these ex-soldiers would persevere, go make some money in the workplace, then succeed with their second businesses, just as Taylor did.

Our wars today don't have Pearl Harbors or Hiroshima to mark their beginnings and ends clearly. Even 9/11 didn't signal that kind of decisive change. Americans had to wait longer at airports and saw many new security measures on roads and in buildings, but within a week, we were back at work in our already booming economy. The attacks on the Twin Towers and the Pentagon happened eighteen years ago. Though those events did lead to a military buildup, none of the new troops would become veterans until a few years later.

Many of our current crop of vets didn't join the military until after 2010, but they are all among the 3.6 million discharged since 2001. Without access to financial resources or mentorship, few vets can start their businesses immediately after discharge. Like their predecessors, they need time, and unlike those children of the Depression, today's vets don't feel as pressured to start their businesses right away. People get married and start families later than they did in the postwar years, so it's no surprise that they also wait until later in life to start new business ventures. No doubt the statistics on veteran start-ups will improve in the next decade.

Some vets are determined to overcome all these hurdles right now. The proportion of women starting businesses after leaving the military is rising quickly. Currently, 16% of America's active-duty military are women. According to figures from the U.S. Census Bureau, the number of businesses owned by women vets quadrupled from 97,000 in 2007 to 383,000 in 2012, and their proportion among all vet entrepreneurs rose from 2.5% to 4.4% in the same period. This trend has been encouraged by government contracting regulations, which now favor women-run businesses.

One of these businesses, a technology start-up called Halfaker and Associates, is owned by Dawn Halfaker, who lost an arm in Iraq. According to Halfaker: "[T]here is no question that my military training has helped me become a better entrepreneur. You go through so much in the military, but really what the military is teaching you is how to be resilient. You plan a mission, and then you execute, but nothing ever goes according to plan. Your job is to continue to lead in not-ideal circumstances."

No doubt, Halfaker realizes that any experienced entrepreneur might describe running a business in the same words.

It's Never Too Soon: Active Duty Entrepreneurship

Though entrepreneurship requires discipline, endurance, and many other qualities of the soldier, in some ways, it's a 180-degree turn from the kind of thinking soldiers do in the military. According to Air Force Colonel, successful entrepreneur, and author Jason C. Anderson, the primary challenge in the transition from the military to business ownership is giving up what he calls: the "military ecosystem." He defines this system in terms of the four major benefits individuals and families receive from it: 1) a steady twice-a-month paycheck 2)

health care for the entire family 3) high job stability, and 4) a predictable career timeline.

Though military personnel and their families may face unexpected deployments, injuries, or even death, in return, the military gives them peace of mind. Paychecks come on time, quality health care is available for service members and their families, and if you stay in for twenty years, some of these benefits go on for life. It's the kind of cradle-to-grave package that many working civilians have always wished for but have seldom found. It's also one big reason why the transition from a military life built on security to an entrepreneurial life built on risk is seldom easy.

"Becoming an entrepreneur takes a lot of time, passion, support, and money," Colonel Anderson writes. "People quickly become overwhelmed for two reasons: they see the task as being too enormous for the undertaking, and don't know how to take the first step."

That first step is the subject of a lot of conversations about entrepreneurship, whether military or any other kind. Your first step might be an application for licensing or an investment pitch. It could even be the simple act of starting your research. Whatever that initial move is, anyone who seriously considers entrepreneurship considers it carefully—in some cases too carefully. They go back over subjects they've already covered, then ask for advice they've already heard. They puzzle endlessly over every question and seldom settle on answers. They imagine resources they don't have, and all the money they might lose if they fail. They picture the potential effects of failure on their families and their other relationships. They look at fallback options and insurance, and no matter how many guarantees and backup plans they can create, there's never enough. With all this reflection going on, potential entrepreneurs can be forgiven if they sometimes lose confidence in themselves and their ideas. As they begin this process, some realize they don't even know what kind of businesses they want to start.

Most of us can imagine all kinds of businesses. At the imagination stage, you might think of yourself as owning and running any company, but then you will see the limitations of reality. You could open a barber shop, a delivery service, or a grocery store, but you would need to learn new skills to do any of these things. You might also need to learn some basic bookkeeping and a few other essential business practices. If you've never done this before, it can look far more daunting than it really is.

If it doesn't look daunting, you might want to do a reality check before you open your business. Few start-ups are easy. If one looks as if it will be, you're probably not considering all the factors. As you made your calculations, did you include all your taxes, licensing fees, a realistic estimate of the required working capital, and the first year of employee benefits? In some cases, going through the motions of starting a business while you're still in active service can help you identify anything you might have missed. You can research, and possibly begin operating your business before you leave active duty. This automatically limits your time, but it also gives you the initial support of a regular paycheck.

In retrospect, Ryan Williams probably should have done something like that. This former Navy SEAL told an interviewer that the process of going from the military structure into free-market entrepreneurship was "incredibly humbling." Williams left active duty in 2008. At the time he was planning an apparel company that he would own with another former SEAL. "We thought we were so cool," he said later, "that we had it all figured out, [but] our egos got smashed very quickly once we started talking to bigger business people who actually owned significant companies."

The first problems arose when they were looking for a print shop that could print Ryan's designs on the

T-shirts the men planned to sell. As the two vets tried to solve the printing problems, more difficulties arose in other areas. Their estimates on shipping and delivery times were far too low, while projected costs were far too high. From their first day, they were running into unanticipated crises right and left. The software didn't work, orders were damaged, and other orders were lost. "A lot of the problems came from us being completely unprepared," Williams later admitted. By that time, he could laugh about his early entrepreneurial errors. In those first days, he did not even know how to export his T-shirt designs to image files: "We would drag out a laptop and show it to them." They settled questions of authority by flipping a coin and had only the vaguest idea of what was in their incorporation documents.

This naiveté couldn't last. These two veterans saw that they were in over their heads, and quickly retreated to their entrepreneurial drawing board.

Eventually, they launched the apparel start-up, Forged Clothing. Now they are finally finding success.

One of the biggest problems Williams faced was how to support himself through the start-up's lean times. Though as a SEAL he was highly qualified for many jobs, the best ones required a lasting commitment. If he was going to start a business, his work there would eventually take up most of his time. With that obligation in mind, Williams couldn't sign a long-term contract. Instead, he took what he could get short-term. It wasn't always much, which only increased the uncertainty of his start-up.

If these men had teamed up and started their business while they were still serving in the military, they might have made their mistakes under much less pressure. They could have done their research, begun a small operation, and they might have even seen a little profit before the business became full-time. Instead, they waited until they got out, quickly realized how ineffective their preparations had been, and were immediately thrown into crisis mode. Their idea was fine, but despite all their work, their business skills needed some sharpening. Fortunately, they had endurance and flexibility. Without these, they would have lost their gamble.

Those who are trained in the planning and execution of military operations know that they can't avoid the element of risk. No battle is won until goals are achieved and the enemy is neutralized. Until one side prevails, failure is possible. No entrepreneur should be afraid of risk. A veteran entrepreneur must regard it as an inevitability and use it to create opportunities. Of course, those opportunities will bring new risks of their own.

Most aspiring entrepreneurs learn that failure is sometimes a necessary prologue to success. This parallels a military school of thought that soldiers learn best from their mistakes. Failure necessitates reevaluation and analysis of what went wrong. If a military operation fails, a commander must examine that failure, identifying the weak points. That's where he or she will find the seeds of future success. That's how wars are won, and it's the foundation of success for many veteran-owned businesses. As Air Force Major Timothy Trimailo wrote recently: "Without risk-taking, there is no return on investment. Military leaders must embody that entrepreneurial spirit in order to seize an opportunity and maintain the ever-changing position of relative advantage over the enemy. On the other hand, the key to effective risk-taking is analysis and prudence. All three of these points illustrate why military leaders must fail early in their careers to be effective organizational leaders at higher echelons."

Marine Corps veteran Nick Koumalatsos recently starred in the Discovery Channel's Trailblazers series. He was on the show because of his efforts as an entrepreneur. Koumalatsos had decided to start a business for two reasons: he enjoyed the process of overcoming obstacles, and he hoped to teach civilians some of the essential lessons he'd learned in the Marines. He began Survival Tactical Systems to teach leadership and tactics to soldiers, police, reservists, and private security teams. The company has been having great success, but it wasn't always like that. "During your first year, you suck," Koumalatsos now says. "Your ideas suck. So you have to adapt and be flexible and evolve."

Like many of the entrepreneurs we've examined here, Koumalatsos began with a good idea, but little knowledge of the business. At first his company struggled, and for a time, Nick doubted whether his start-up would make it. Gradually he recognized that he had only a vague sense of his company's mission, or how to measure success. He pulled back, reassessed, and then returned to his project rejuvenated. The experience left him with a new respect for flexibility. He'd reinvented his business with a much clearer sense of how to execute his original idea. "I feel like I succeed and fail every day," Koumalatsos told a reporter. "You have to own up to the decisions you make. There are things I've done better today than yesterday. You just need to focus on putting one foot in front of the other."

When Koumalatsos went back to his drawing board, he found himself creating a much more focused picture of the things he should have been doing before: teaching civilians the survival skills, teamwork, and leadership he'd learned in the Marines. Once he'd restarted his business, he got a loan from StreetShares.com, allowing him to grow his business while still providing high-quality service to his existing clientele. StreetShares, which announces itself as "Proudly Veteran-Run," was happy to help a former Marine like Koumalatsos. They were instantly drawn to a start-up based on the same kinds of training and fellowship that one finds in the military.

Now in its second time around, Survival Tactical Systems is doing well, and Koumalatsos hopes for a bright future. "When you have time to think about it and work through it, you'll always come back stronger," he says.

Another Marine Corps veteran, who is also a firefighter and an entrepreneur, is Zachary Green. Green had a great idea, plenty of passion, but little backing. He'd heard that New York City had enacted a fire safety law requiring structures that were over three stories high to have guidance in hallways and stairwells. This meant these buildings would need strips of treated tape and other photoluminescent devices to illuminate smoky areas and guide firefighters through their missions.

Green tested his first iteration on the job. It was a photoluminescent band fitted onto his helmet. It was so good at lighting up darkened areas that it was an immediate hit with his fellow firefighters. Over the next six months, he sold $5,000 worth of helmet bands, mostly out of the trunk of his car. This was the promising, yet shaky start of MN8 Foxfire.

Green's difficulty was in maintaining enough cash flow to keep his fledgling business alive. Soon he had maxed out all his credit cards, remortgaged his house, and risked his entire financial life and that of his family. "I never got scared in the Marines or the fire department," Green says, "but entrepreneurship is the scariest thing ever." He persevered, found funding to cover his cash flow shortfalls, and eventually became one of today's most successful veteran entrepreneurs. "Building and growing MN8 has been more difficult than I could have ever imagined, but all things worth having are also worth fighting for," Green wrote in a later blog post.

Green had a singular idea, which was almost like a vision. His idea grew from the life-threatening situations he and his firefighting colleagues faced every day. This kind of idea is the entrepreneur's inspiration, and a business that succeeds from this inspiration is often the only business this entrepreneur would ever start. He might try, fail, and try again, but if he reaches the success, it will be because of his dedication to the idea that originally inspired him.

Some potential business owners spend a lot of time puzzling over ideas. After all, shouldn't the first consideration be the purpose of the start-up? That only sounds like common sense, and it's often true. A business must provide something people will pay for, but that leaves the door open to an infinite number of possibilities. Like Green, there are some entrepreneurs who have always known what kind of businesses they want to start. Williams liked iconic T-shirt art and wanted to make money creating his own designs. Koumalatsos felt that military leadership and methods could be successfully applied to civilian security. A good cook might dream of owning her own restaurant, while a math whiz may feel destined to open an accounting service. Carpenters yearn to be contractors, writers want to be publishers, and the ditch digger is saving to start a landscaping service. Finally, there are many others who have strong entrepreneurial ambitions but feel stymied by the fact that they don't have a single specific idea for a business.

Though it might seem that starting a business requires the entrepreneur to have a great passion for the subject of that business (the idea), that's not always true. Some people develop their personal interest in a business only after they've started it. Prior to that, these business owners invested their time and money simply based on profit. How could they possibly succeed without a real passion for the actual service or product? How could they remain focused, or find enough energy? The answer is that they have a strong passion for entrepreneurship itself. They enjoy all the challenges of starting an enterprise—almost any enterprise—and getting it off the ground. They specialize in putting businesses on a solid footing. After that, such an entrepreneur might stick with it, but he or she is far more likely to hire someone else to run it or to sell it for a profit. When this happens, entrepreneurs are like winning generals leaving the battlefield to reap honors and promotions. They've conquered and held the territory, and now others can do the necessary work of running it.

Colonel Anderson doesn't accept any excuses about the lack of ideas for a start-up. He writes: "One of the biggest misconceptions military members have regarding entrepreneurship is that they must have an idea to begin. While having an idea is certainly preferable, it is by no means a requirement . . . Entrepreneurship is all about making yourself available to new opportunities. So, whether you have an idea or not, it is important to try to change your environment."

Staff Sergeant Alan Pruitt has succeeded in several entrepreneurial ventures while still in the military. In operating these businesses, he's adapted his military skills to civilian purposes. His civilian businesses have included start-ups in real estate sales, finance, and other specialized areas. He reminds soldiers that their time in the service is a chance to earn credentials for these kinds of things. "Pursue professional certifications that are knowledge-based," Pruitt says. He suggests that soldiers earn credentials in fields like real estate, personal training, accounting, or "anything healthcare related . . . Choose certifications that are portable (recognized anywhere in the US); professionally accepted and offer the chance at possible self-employment. As hockey legend Wayne Gretzky said, 'I skate to where the puck is going to be, not where it has been.' Take his advice and apply it to your current and future business (and career) plans."

Though you might not know at this point what business you want to start, you should focus on possibilities to which you feel a strong attraction. When interviewed by the reporter Geoff Weiss about what potential entrepreneurs need, several experienced veteran-entrepreneurs agreed that one necessity was some kind of plan. Good experience and intentions can count for a lot, but only if they have a purpose. A good plan can channel the veteran's talents and skills toward achieving this purpose.

Weiss tells the story of a Navy SEAL who visited the office of Eric Eversole. Eversole is the executive director of Hiring Our Heroes, a federal program aimed at connecting vets with employers. The vet had one of the best resumes Eversole had ever seen, so the director asked the man: "Ultimately, what do you want to do?"

"To lead," the vet replied.

The answer's force and brevity make it appear to be an eloquent and inspiring response, but as Eversole knew, the man was ignoring the critical importance of identifying his mission. "You'd never just automatically jump into a hot zone without a plan," he later told Weiss. This eager yet unfocused vet might have benefited from trying a start-up while still on active duty. Such an effort might have allowed him to learn from his mistakes while still having his military paycheck to fall back on.

Many service members avoid active-duty start-ups due to their vague fear of violating military regulations. They don't know the rules, so they give up before they start. Some older service members subscribe to a general attitude that says soldiers should limit their business activity to stocks, bonds, and other "passive" investments. This attitude is coupled with a mistaken impression that the military discourages most active-duty start-ups. That's not true. Though the rules on military entrepreneurship emphasize that the service member's military commitments must always come first, our government has programs that encourage active-duty start-ups. The Small Business Administration (SBA) has several military-friendly programs, and the Defense and Agriculture departments offer loan packages specifically designed for service members, whether active or not.

Former Army Captain Ian Folau is an author and a successful venture capitalist. He advocates entrepreneurship as the best route to success, even while a service member is still on active duty. Folau has considered the oft-recommended alternative of passive investments, but this route doesn't hold any attraction for him.

"Some [service members] believe that the only way to supplement their income is to invest in stocks, real estate, or their TSP," Folau tells readers. "I don't find the justification there in saying that I can put effort into researching and buying real estate, then renovating and managing that property, but I can't put my own effort into anything else that could make me money. If I had $2,000 to invest, and I was a young serviceman with plenty of time left in my mortal existence, I would not simply get into the betting game of investing in stocks. [It] does not allow you to put in your own effort in order to increase the value of your investment, something we call 'sweat equity.'

"I would look at providing a service or product that others would pay me money for. One approach to providing a service is to think of something that you are passionate about, and less than 5% of the people you know have in-depth experience with. This could be car detailing, fantasy basketball, model airplanes, or watch collecting."

Folau advises young, entrepreneurial-minded service members to take interests like these and create websites around them to test the waters. He recommends that a service member take this step while still on active duty. It can prepare the service member for creating a start-up after discharge, or for opening a business even while he or she is still a full-time soldier. Starting such a website is your first step in developing the "sweat equity" Folau has mentioned. "This site [must] provide awesome content that either people can't find anywhere else, or have a unique perspective," he says. "Match the site up with social media and draw as many people as possible. You start making money by providing links to companies on your site."

Folau's idea can be applied to almost any field. You might create a site concentrating on car repair. You start with basics, but you also give the site a unique viewpoint. Your content might look at the future of car repair as the automotive world goes electric. Or you might go in the opposite direction and dedicate your site to the restoration and repair of antique vehicles. Whatever you do, make sure your site is inviting, appealing, and memorable. Look for related sites, and then use social media to expand your audience. Take advantage of every opportunity to increase traffic and find advertisers.

Folau believes that creating such a website is one way to jump-start your business while you're still on active duty. It gives you a way to take a general idea, and test details and methods before you begin investing money and seeking backers. In your interactions with visitors, you will learn what's in demand, and why they want it. When it's time to put your full service online or open a bricks-and-mortar shop or office, what you've learned from your website experience will help you refine your ideas and avoid many rookie errors.

A site like this might begin producing profits on its own. If you can stand out from the crowd, you might attract enough hits to make real money on the advertising. This could help you fund your actual business, or it might even become your actual business.

Folau points out that almost all active-duty entrepreneurs face the same question: "Do you want to have this business take over your life and be your primary source of income at some point, or do you just want to make some quick money?" He admits that his own active-duty business was more for the immediate money than for any future profit potential. He says his main goal was to learn. "I was fine doing business for the sake of experience," he writes. "I didn't want to lose money, but as long as I broke even, I felt like I had gained a bunch of lessons for free. It wasn't until I left the army, that I decided to make entrepreneurship my primary source of income. But by then, I felt I was ready for it."

As we've already seen, some start-up ideas simply don't work. Your online sports equipment store doesn't attract any customers, or you can't find reliable workers for your office cleaning service. If this happens, Sergeant Pruitt advises: "Fail fast. That's my go-to phrase for anyone seeking my small business start-up advice. Some ideas are just that—ideas. Don't get trapped into being a financial martyr for an idea that will drain you and your loved ones financially and emotionally."

This fits neatly with Captain Folau's recommendation about starting a website that relates to your future business. Don't spend much of your hard-earned pay on design. Find a simple, straightforward, and attractive template and see what you can do yourself. Though the task may seem scary at first, if you persevere you will find that you are learning new digital skills without even realizing it. Study ways to use social media to drive traffic to your site, and learn how to create content that keeps them there. To begin producing revenue, start running those ads. Look into the advertising services of Google, Amazon, and other online giants. They have many packages, and once people start clicking on the ads, you can get a small percentage of what they spend at those sites. That will be your company's first revenue.

You can start this kind of business for free, though you will have to invest your time, attention, and energy. If you start a site and soon realize it's a flop, then it's time to follow Sergeant Pruitt's dictum, and "fail fast." You won't be losing much money, and if you've learned something of value, then your time and effort aren't wasted. Once you've analyzed what went wrong, use what you've learned to create another, better website. If you come up with one that produces profits, then your small business is already up and running. If you then expand it into a bricks-and-mortar shop or service, you will already have a thriving website to give you a head start.

Starting your business while still on active duty can be a smart, sensible choice. Even if it doesn't make money, you will learn from the experience, and be better prepared for the future. If it is profitable, you will have solved the problem of what to do after your discharge: you will have created your own job.

WHEN WOMEN TAKE CHARGE: TODAY'S VETERAN WOMEN AND ENTREPRENEURSHIP

Whether we are on active duty or are settled into civilian life, each of us has a unique combination of talents, skills, and traits. When we look for work, we search for jobs that match our abilities. Sometimes the perfect job is waiting, but most of the time we must take what's offered. One advantage in a start-up is that the entrepreneur has an opportunity to design her own job. She can tailor it to exploit her talents and compensate in areas where she might be weak. This process occurs in the entrepreneur's first act of job creation: hiring herself.

Dajon Ferrell had served in the Public Affairs and Marketing division of the Army. "I thought the military was going to be a career for me," Dajon told an interviewer. "When I got out and looked at people my age doing that 9-to-5 life, I thought, 'Okay, so I'm going to make X amount, not really feel like I have much control over my time, and not really feel like I have a purpose? No, thanks, I'll do it on my own.'"

Dajon wanted to help others, but she wanted control of her work and schedule. She became an empowerment coach. Dajon works with both veterans and civilians. She specializes in helping people afflicted by problems she's experienced herself: anxiety, depression, or PTSD. Her job also includes work with victims of sexual trauma. She created a brand for herself: The Mindful Veteran. It's a way to continue her service in an entrepreneurial firm. "When you get out of the military, it's hard to just go into a daily-grind mode," Dajon told one questioner. "You really seek that challenge and a way to still be of service."

Dajon represents one of the fastest-growing sectors of entrepreneurship: start-ups founded by women veterans. According to a survey of entrepreneurs conducted by the Census Bureau, the number of vet-owned businesses increased by about 10% between 2007 and 2012. Virtually the entire increase came from new businesses that were majority-owned by women vets. These were up by 296%. All in all, this was enough to make up for the 7% drop in male veteran-owned start-ups in the same years. Carla Harris, chair of the National Women's Business Council, told a reporter: "The growth of veteran women entrepreneurship has been higher than any other segment of the entrepreneurship economy."

Some of the statistics for women aren't so obviously rosy. Despite the near-quadrupling of women veteran-owned businesses, the combined receipts of these companies have risen only 26%. This suggests that many of these start-ups were temporary projects or business ventures with their own automatic limitations. Most of these companies were created to make money quickly, then end, such as brief opportunities in door-to-door cosmetic sales, or businesses that were set up to liquidate inventory and equipment on a onetime basis. These kinds of temporary businesses weren't designed for growth. They are small-scale activities targeting specific purposes, though they could be redesigned to become real companies with the potential to grow. "We have to shift the focus to scaling these businesses," says Amanda Brown of the National Women's Business Council. "Even if you are in a lifestyle business, there are ways to grow and scale that."

Women vets face the same sexism and skepticism as civilian women, but in the military culture, where they still make up only 16% of the workforce, they can sometimes feel more isolated. Because this isolation often persists through her whole career, a female vet might not know where to turn when she gets out. That's why Shelley Rood, a former Army all-source tactical-intelligence officer, and member of Detroit's WeWork Campus Martius in Detroit, created Missilia as a community for "women who kick butt." "When I read the statistic that 42% of female veterans don't feel respected and valued, I knew I had to do something to help bring them together," she told one reporter.

Rood, a former captain with sixteen years in the service, is not alone in her concern. When the veteran nonprofit, The Mission Continues, surveyed a cross-section of female vets, only 37% reported that they felt "recognized, respected, and valued as veterans in civilian life." "As a military veteran, I'm highly capable in so many ways—but I've had multiple corporate experiences and management jobs where I was often underutilized in order to fit the job description," says Rood.

Rood's organization is dedicated to the recognition of the value of strong women. Her typical audiences are women firefighters, entrepreneurs, security professionals, and, of course, veterans. They are all seeking the same thing: a support community to help strong women grow even stronger. "[That's] what I decided to create," Rood says. While her Missilia site highlights extraordinary women, it also features natural beauty products, healthy snacks, and effective self-defense tools. The text on the site celebrates independent women and encourages visitors to put their creativity to work. "In the military, you're entrusted with high-risk, high-stakes situations and told, 'Figure it out,'" says Rood. "And they won't accept excuses. You have to think outside the box."

Another support organization for veteran women, people of color, and those in the nonconforming community is Minority Veterans of America (MVA). The group was started by Lindsey Church, who served in the Navy as a linguist. She wanted to connect with other minority vets so that they could create a community where their voices would be heard. Her organization serves underrepresented veterans nationwide. At the one-year mark, MVA has six hundred members, and four thousand followers on Facebook. "As a female veteran, I almost never saw female veterans," she says. "As a gender-nonconforming veteran, I felt like the only one in the room. And I realized, within the veteran community, I saw no people of color, no religious minorities. But I got so sick of complaining about it; I just wanted to do something about it."

Church's organization is also linked with WeWork, an organization dedicated to helping vets adapt to the civilian world. WeWork has teamed with a nonprofit promoter of veteran entrepreneurship, Bunker Labs, to help veterans who are interested in making this adjustment as entrepreneurs. These organizations have created the Veterans in Residence program, which concentrates on helping vets who are doing start-ups. Though women make up 16% of military personnel, the proportion of aspiring women entrepreneurs in Veterans in Residence is nearly double that—three out of ten.

"For a long time, the narrative has been that veterans are straight, white, Christian men," Church told a recent interviewer, "but as more women join the military—and more become vets—there's more recognition happening for female veterans. We've been here all along, but we're starting to be welcomed to the table, which is changing what we're capable of doing."

Many women vets experience hardships in their shift to civilian life. After discharge, quite a few of them start their own companies because they can't find regular jobs. They wait longer before applying for benefits, and after leaving the service, they often need a lot more time to find full-time work. Women vets have unusually high unemployment rates. Data from a study done by Syracuse University shows the total female veteran unemployment rate from 2008 to 2012 was 11.1%, 4% higher than that of women. The younger a woman is, the worse it gets. One recent survey found that women vets between the ages of twenty and twenty-four were unemployed at a rate of 35.4%.

One explanation for the growth in women vet entrepreneurs is the rising number of women in military service. The fastest growing post-9/11 veteran demographic is that of women, and while more are starting new businesses, some others find nothing but trouble as they enter the civilian ranks. As more and more women leave the military, they run a greater risk of homelessness and joblessness than they ever have before. In a 2017 report to Congress, the U.S. Department of Housing and Urban Development (HUD) gave a single-night estimate of over four thousand women veterans living on the streets. In the previous year, the homeless female veteran population had jumped 7%, while the rate among male vets had increased only 1%. The National Center on Homelessness Among Veterans puts the number of homeless women veterans at 36,443, or triple that of just five years earlier.

James Schmeling, the co-founder of the Institute for Veterans and Military Families at Syracuse University, notes that more female vets have parenting duties, which hinders their efforts to get and keep a job. Also, sexism and male-based traditions make it harder for women to find opportunities to apply what they've learned in the military to civilian purposes. Schmeling's Institute addresses this, and many other veteran start-up issues, with education and training programs for business-minded veterans. The Institute's offerings include the SBA's Operation Boots to Business program, the Entrepreneurship Bootcamp for Veterans with Disabilities, and Veteran Women Igniting the Spirit of Entrepreneurship program.

"We've put about 39,000 people through [our programs]," says Schmeling. "Part of what we do is educate them on access to capital, financing their business or bootstrapping a business."

The one-woman vet who was doing the balancing act between start-up work and family duties was Beth

Graeme of Mechanicsville, Maryland. As a Navy veteran, Beth's first civilian job seemed like a good fit. Her employer was servicing the same classes of ships Graeme had known in the Navy. At the time, her husband was still deployed overseas, and Graeme's job often conflicted with her family duties. "With a full household of kids, it was hard to be the only person here and manage everything and have a full-time job," she later told an interviewer. Unfortunately, her workplace was also infected with sexism. "Being a female in an all-male shop, I kind of got these eyes on me when I had to take time off for child care purposes," she now says.

Graeme thought about shifting to part-time work, but then realized she would still face some of the same problems. Her kids might need her anytime, and Graeme was determined to be there for them. "I needed to get out of a place where I felt like being a girl wasn't accepted," she now says. The only solution was to create her own job—one she could do from home.

Finally, in 2012, Graeme took the plunge. Grambo Creative was born, offering photography and design services. This one-woman show produced income almost from the start. It didn't grow much at first, but Graeme didn't want it to. Only recently did she finally hire two part-time employees. She wants to build slowly, and won't take a step until she's truly ready. She has this luxury because, as she puts it: "[Now] whenever I need to make money, I make it."

The classification of your business can make a difference. If you are trying to qualify for government contracts, some classifications will be better for women, others for people of color, and still others will encourage applications from vets. If you qualify for multiple classifications, and only one is available, which one should you choose?

That was one of the many choices Tabatha Turman faced as she was starting Integrated Finance and Accounting Solutions LLC (IFAS). Though her company is 100% woman-owned, it's also 100%

veteran-owned. She could apply for either classification. Knowing that she would be dealing with the Defense Department and its contractors, Turman found that her company's veteran-owned status brought the best advantages. It helped her jump over some hurdles when pursuing contracts. She's not so sure about getting a certification as a woman-owned business. There will be other cases where she will have to decide which certification to use, and so far, she hasn't seen any advantages in the women's certifications that would outweigh those of her vet-owned status.

Turman has met other women vets who are aspiring entrepreneurs, and when she asks about their military work, she's always surprised. "They had these huge jobs," she says, yet the businesses they are starting are often small ventures, seemingly lacking in ambition and vision. She thinks of these little businesses (usually designed for slow growth or none) as little more than hobbies. Turman is more interested in those who are willing to work to achieve big dreams. She urges women vets who are thinking of becoming entrepreneurs to try government contracting. It's one way to design your business for growth. "You are on the cusp of something brilliant if you just go that extra mile," she told one reporter.

Turman began her entrepreneurship as an accountant working from her own kitchen table. She was working part-time and had only a few clients. At a workshop in 2007, Turman met the person who gave her an initial consulting subcontract. That was the beginning. Soon there were more clients and contracts. These eventually grew into Turman's IFAS, a company that sells its accounting and financial services to the government. IFAS now has about $10 million in annual revenue and employs over one hundred people.

Brooke Jones-Chinetti had been in the military herself, graduating from West Point in 2009. While serving her country, Brooke formed bonds with her fellow soldiers, and gained a keen appreciation of the value of comradeship and sacrificing for others. Her colleagues in the Army always watched out for her, and she automatically did the same for them. She was always willing to lend an ear or go the extra mile to solve a problem.

Brooke married another Army officer, but soon they decided that two active service members in a family were one too many. Conflicts between postings, work orders, schedules, and childcare seemed inevitable. One of them might have stayed in, but soon the couple decided that their plans would stand a better chance of success if both separated from the military.

Brooke was discharged first, but she soon found that it was hard to replace the feeling of fellowship and purpose that had been a part of the air she breathed in the Army. She longed for a mentor or anyone who would listen and understand what she was feeling. That's what got her started on Your Sequel.

Your Sequel is a network open to any of the forty thousand women who separate from the service every year. This platform is a clearinghouse where women vets can air their ideas and experiences about all the issues they face in this process. It fosters encouragement rather than competition and provides information that's essential to women who want to make educated choices about the future.

"The military is such a strong community where everyone has each other's back," Brooke told a recent interviewer. "When you leave that, you can feel very vulnerable. When women empower other women, it's revolutionary. [D]on't tear each other down to build yourself up. When you see someone struggling, extend a hand to help."

It's good advice for anyone, and particularly apt for veterans starting businesses. They know that if they need help, their fellow vets will be there.

Married to the Military: Military Spouses and Entrepreneurship

When Jocelyn Velaquez married a career Army infantryman, she wasn't expecting to need a job right away. "I was getting my degree in accounting, so that I could have a job when he retired," Velaquez later told an interviewer. But once she had her undergraduate degree, she soon tired of life without real work. She began looking for whatever job she could find, but even after months of searching, she still had no full-time options.

By a year later, Velaquez and her husband became parents, and they needed a second paycheck. "I was worried about not being able to find a job and not only that but child care," Velaquez says. Lowering her sights, she started looking for part-time work. She was ready to do almost anything that would bring in some cash. She was putting in a couple of shifts each week at a tanning salon when she found a freelance entrepreneurial option that would let her work from home. It involved cutting leather for handbags. The company would send her the leather, and she would be paid by the piece. This not only solved her childcare problem, but it also gave her portability, allowing her to take her job with her wherever she might go. For a military spouse, this was not just welcome—it was essential.

Military spouses have always been caught in this bind. About 88% of military spouses are women. No matter what sex you are, marriage to a service member can often mean uprooting yourself and your work whenever your spouse is reassigned. The average military family moves once every 2.9 years. Sometimes these moves take them to remote bases where there are few civilians and fewer job opportunities. Even when a military spouse finds herself in a big city, she's not likely to find the kind of work that fits her qualifications. Who wants to hire someone who's likely to quit as soon as her spouse gets new orders?

Problems like these have pushed the unemployment rate among military spouses to 26%. That's not 26% of all military spouses—just those who are actively seeking work. If you are married to someone in the military, and you want to provide that second paycheck for your family, the chances are better than one in four that you won't be able to do it. Eighty-five percent of military spouses are looking for jobs. For most of them, it's a necessity, yet thousands of these spouses will fail.

One study done by the nonprofit, Blue Star Families (BSF) says that "75% of active duty spouses reported being a military spouse had a negative impact on their ability to pursue employment." Cristin Orr Shiffer, Senior Advisor of Policy and Survey for BSF, told a reporter: "[I]t's a structural problem around the spouses . . . there are no jobs in their specific field in the area they live, no job openings of any type, or [they] lack the qualifications for the jobs that are open." Shiffer added that the inability of military spouses to move where the jobs are—as many of their civilian competitors do—further aggravates the problem.

Of the million-plus current military spouses, 63% are married to active-duty service members, while 37% are wed to soldiers in the reserves. As we've noted, almost nine out of ten of these spouses are women. Though they all share the same military- marital status, these spouses have diverse talents and skills. The problem is they seldom get to use them.

Over 90% of the spouses who have succeeded in finding jobs have been judged to be overqualified, yet they feel that they should be given more work, even entry-level positions. Though these spouses have more training, education, and experience than they need for the jobs they're applying for, they are so eager to work that they just don't care. Even though their qualifications and experience might seem wasted, they'll take whatever they can find. Most of these spouses are now reduced to filling their résumés with the same kinds of short-term employment an industrious high school student might have. Some spouses don't even include their part-time work as adults. When employers look at an adult's résumé, they want to see evidence of longevity and responsibility. If a grown person lists the kinds of fleeting low-wage gigs he or she has been working, a prospective employer will often see those as red flags.

Among today's military-spouse entrepreneurs, some are creating businesses aimed at helping other military spouses navigate the difficulties they face. That's what Army wife, Leigh Searl is doing. As an Army spouse, Leigh knows the problems other job-seeking spouses confront. In her first fourteen years of marriage, she moved eleven times and had two children. Throughout these years she found no use for her law degree (which she earned from one of the nation's best law schools). Searl desperately wanted worthwhile work, but she was moving every fifteen months. When she finally began to find some suitable freelance options, the jobs she came up with had one thing in common: they were tasks she could do from her desk at home. This was the seed of the idea that would soon become America's Career Force.

Searl wanted her start-up to help other military spouses find jobs they could do remotely with an internet connection. She designed America's Career Force website to encourage communications between well-educated and highly-trained military spouses and employers who are ready to hire them. In doing this, Searl has discovered just how hidden this problem is. Many employers know nothing about the high unemployment rates of military spouses, nor are they aware of this vast global pool of potential talent. Searl has begun to educate them about the situation, and their potential to benefit from it. She's been so effective that even Fortune 500 companies are hiring her candidates. These people are doing well, and if Searl can keep finding jobs for them, she'll be a part of a movement that will ultimately change the way America's companies think of military spouses. Up until now if a company's strategy took military spouses into consideration, it was only as consumers. Today these companies are learning that these spouses are also producers.

One of the military spouses whose entrepreneurship targets others like herself is Jennifer Pilcher. Pilcher is the owner of Strategic Military Communications, LLC, and more recently she founded MilitaryOneClick. Her husband served in the Navy for well over twenty years. During those decades Jennifer pulled up stakes and moved countless times. In the process, she learned firsthand about the unique issues affecting military families.

One issue Pilcher had come up against again and again was how little useful information she could find on these issues. A primary feature of military families is that they move all the time, yet women like Jennifer—the ones who organized and executed most of these moves—had no good source of up-to-date information about local schools, stores, churches, or public facilities in their new postings. What she could find was incomplete, and often out-of-date. After more than two decades of this, Jennifer had seen enough. That's when she inaugurated her own effort to fill this void: Strategic Military Communications LLC. When she designed her company's website, she posted a page of well-organized links designed for military families. That page has evolved into MilitaryOneClick. Here military spouses can find a treasure trove of pertinent information about their next PCS (Permanent Change of Station).

Since she started her entrepreneurial venture, Jennifer has expanded the available data to include tips on moving companies, pets, health care, housing, and children's activities. Today her website's coverage even goes beyond that, offering advice about careers and finances, and news relating to military life.

The website has even made Jennifer into somewhat of a celebrity. In the last days of the Obama administration, she represented our nation's military spouses at a White House gathering that highlighted the roles of military moms and kids. The event's organizers selected Jennifer to introduce First Lady Michelle Obama, and Dr. Jill Biden, spouse of Vice President Joe Biden. In her introductions, Jennifer made special mention of these women's work on issues that concern military moms.

With all this concentration on moms, what about their children? One Army spouse, Amy Crispino, was ready to address this demographic. She called her initial start-up: Chameleon Kids. The name refers to military kids' ability to pick up and move so often. These kids must adapt to new and strange environments all the time. In doing so, they learn how to fit into new surroundings, much like a color-changing chameleon blends in with any landscape where he might find himself.

Chameleon Kids was essentially an information site, so it wasn't much of a jump to create a hard copy magazine. Recently Amy published the first issue of *Military Kids' Life Magazine*. This magazine isn't just for kids; it's even by kids. They write over half the content. Already it is proving to be a huge success. In another recent development, Amy and her company won a StreetShares award given to the nation's best small businesses owned by veterans. She's using the money to develop new journalism programs that will encourage kids to write. She wants them to get a real journalistic experience.

One thing that's common to all these examples is the idea of cooperation. We live in a country and culture that celebrate the competition. Our games, financial systems, and even our method of government all involve competing with others. Competition can be a very productive force, but it can also arouse passions that are hard to control. Unless competition is tempered by compassion, it won't produce the best outcomes.

These women don't overemphasize the competitive aspects of a business. They feel that competition is such an obvious feature of business that it doesn't need any further explanation. They believe in winning, but they have no urge to see others lose. They want everyone to win in the best way possible. Leigh Searl wants to help her fellow spouses find rewarding work, while Jennifer Pilcher gives them tips on their endless moves. Amy Crispino is teaching kids the same cooperative spirit.

Though R.Riveter sells a physical product (handbags), it is yet another business that thrives on the spirit of cooperation. This is the company that contracted with Jocelyn Velaquez to cut leather for its handbags. Its co-founder and CEO, Lisa Bradley, notes: "As a military spouse, you're moving around every 2.9 years, so it's really difficult to find long-term employment and something that can not only [give you] employment but something that you can take with you and something you can grow in." These words hardly sound like they could come from a cutthroat competitor. Bradley knows her cooperative freelance workforce. She's one of them.

Currently, Velaquez lives in Colorado Springs, where her husband serves at Fort Carson. She started cutting leather for handbags three years ago when her spouse was stationed in Georgia. With a husband and five children to manage, Velaquez is a great example of how the R.Riveter company is meant to work. She's continued working through two moves now, and she's avoided the undue stress that job concerns can inflict on a military lifestyle.

"I absolutely love it," she told a reporter. "I was surprised I could make this money while working from home . . . The best part is that I always felt guilty if I wanted to work and leave the kids [in] daycare because they do miss out on their dad so much just because of the Army. Even though there are times when they get to see him, I don't want them to miss out on both of their parents. So being able to be home and work and take care of the kids and make sure they have everything they need is a blessing."

Velaquez learned her job quickly, and easily adjusted to its rhythms. No matter where her husband's postings take them, she follows the same pattern. Each month a hide of leather arrives. From this she will cut several pieces, measuring, cutting, and punching holes in the straps. She then sends these pieces to another "riveter" (the company nickname for its freelance workers) who sews it all together; then it makes one last stop with a finisher. "It's all hand-made, and from all that hole punching, my right arm is bigger than my left arm," Velaquez told the reporter. "I haven't figured out the left hand yet."

Most employers would consider Velaquez to be overqualified for this work. She's a college graduate with a bachelor's degree in accounting. But she likes her flexible schedule, and the close relationships she's formed with her coworkers. "We form relationships with women we've never even met," she said. "Another leather girl lives in Oklahoma, and we talk almost every day. We talk about work but also about life and our kids, and we've never met. We're close because we all understand the military lifestyle . . . My husband just got back from a deployment in October, and I was pregnant the whole time. I was bored and going a bit crazy, but the work I do with R.Riveter made the days fly by. It took my mind off worrying."

R.Riveter's owners recently made a successful visit to TV's *Shark Tank*. Their appearance on the show gave them the kind of exposure that led to a dramatic rise in sales. "I used to send in a shipment to be assembled every two months, and now I send in a shipment every week," Velaquez says.

Bradley and her co-owner, Cameron Cruse, understand perfectly why a trained accountant like Velaquez would want to do this instead of the work her education had prepared her for. Bradley and Cruse both had graduate degrees when they started making handbags. They were both trained for specific professions, but handbags proved the better option. Both women have relished this opportunity to start a new kind of business.

In all these ventures, we see military spouses rewriting the rules of running a business. They cooperate instead of competing, move instead of staying put, and even though they're breaking the rules, they are succeeding!

Why Veteran Start-ups Help Us All: America's Best Business Owner

After World War II, millions of soldiers returned to America, dreaming of a job, a family, and owning a home. This made sense. In those days, most Americans simply wanted security. They'd lived through sixteen years of poverty and war, and now they wanted to step out from the shadows of those fears and raise a generation of children who would never know those horrors. If they could get steady work at decent pay, and find an affordable house, that was all they needed to make their own American Dream come true.

Though half of them started businesses, most of these were sidelines to their regular jobs. They thought of these sideline businesses as ways to make money to pay for the house. The house was an investment any veteran could understand; it sheltered them and their families, provided a ready line of credit, and once the mortgage was paid, they had the security of owning something that had substantial value. Real estate prices tended to increase a little faster than inflation, so that value usually went up slowly and surely. For risk-averse vets, it was an easy choice.

Today we live in a more dynamic world. The economy is booming, and while real estate prices are still going up, a house doesn't have the financial potential that a business has. A corner store could become a chain, or a website might gain sudden popularity. At that point, the profits might start flooding in, and a relatively poor veteran can become rich overnight. That veteran might then buy a house, or even two houses, with one that's only used for vacations. Therefore, entrepreneurship is replacing home ownership as Americans' main route to wealth, and veterans are pioneers on that path.

Veterans are some of America's best business owners. Their training, skills, and can-do attitude give them a huge advantage. Almost all veterans have some training in the skills of leadership. They understand its value and can usually provide the inspiration their employees need.

In today's armed forces, soldiers are trained to recognize people's differences. They learn how to work with men and women of every conceivable background. Most soldiers—even those who never rose above private—have some understanding of how to keep discipline while maintaining respect for employees. The most likely soldiers to become entrepreneurs are the self-starters. They will employ a lot of their fellow vets—mostly those vets whose ambitions are more modest, or who simply require more guidance. Now, these former soldiers who protected our country so well will team up again to provide their fellow citizens with products and services for our daily lives.

Michael Crean created such a team, hiring a high percentage of his fellow vets for his start-up. Crean spent almost nine years in the Army and is now the founder and CEO of Solutions Granted. Based in Woodbridge, Virginia, the company advises businesses and government agencies on IT and the newest methods for keeping information secure. They also have security options for just about any online security task, large or small.

Crean is the son of two GM workers. Neither of his parents displayed any great desire to start a business, but their persistence and tenacity in providing for their family made a strong impression on their son. Crean has a talent for leadership, which has shown itself in his military career, and now serves him in the business world. He has achieved great success through leadership, and he recently opened to a reporter about the subject. "[E]veryone who's served in the military can say that they've had people role-model some good leadership styles. Many people may have merely wanted to serve for a single enlistment to earn veterans' education benefits. These veterans may not have become noncommissioned officers, but they did get to learn from and observe many of them. If they become business owners after completing their educations, they'll still have that as an advantage."

Crean's entrepreneurial streak showed up as early as junior high school. He realized he could buy Little Debbie snacks at the store, then bring them into a school where he would sell them for a profit to his friends. Flashes of the entrepreneurial spirit continued to appear through his school career and throughout his years in the military. He considered a career in the Army, but he soon tired of living so much of his life away from his growing family. More than once, Crean left a newborn at home as he deployed to one of the world's troubled spots. Fifteen months later, he would return to a "walking, talking child." He had served his country for almost a decade, and now he wanted to come home and figure out what to do with the rest of his life. He describes what happened next as "a story of dumb luck and needing a job."

About a year after he left the service, Crean was at a job interview when a company representative asked him if he knew anything about computers. "I knew I could learn anything I put my mind to," Crean later recalled, "but I also get bored really easily. The government contracting world puts you in a box, and you do that job for as long as that contract goes on. So, I decided to step out into commercial space. I was valuable because of my leadership qualities."

It was 1999, and Crean was making a vain attempt to outrace the wave of failure that burst the dot-com bubble. "It caught up with me," he said later. "I was mad and disappointed in myself because I'd given up a military career, and now, I was on unemployment."

After putting out feelers for any full-time jobs that might be out there, Crean started getting some calls, but the callers' only interest was in hiring him for specific digital tasks. "A general contracting company offered me a job to tear things down. At the same time, a good friend who worked at a collection agency asked me to build computers and networks . . . Another person [called to say] their full time IT guy left and asked me if I would do it part-time. I would do whatever it took to feed my family . . . That was around 2001, and it just went on from there."

Though Crean credits "dumb luck" for his success, it's clear that luck was only a part of it. He couldn't have done it without the training and confidence the military had given him. He'd learned about computers in the Army, and it was there that he'd sharpened his leadership skills. By 2001 he'd begun Solutions Granted to service customers with needs in cybersecurity and IT. Since then the company has grown bigger than Crean ever dreamed it would.

Did Crean's military experience make him a better businessman? He thinks so. "The things I did in the military—not having running water or eating a meal that comes from a brown plastic bag—taught me to get creative," he now says. "As a business owner, that really lets me know what's important in life. I don't take things that seriously because I know what the military goes through. In my business, what we're doing is important, but no one's going to die today. The military gave perspective. And adaptability! The military taught me that! How to adapt and overcome in the face of adversity. Entrepreneurs need to have this too."

Crean gave his interviewer one last word of advice for vets, or any other entrepreneurs: "Don't worry about all the noise around you. It will become distracting. When you discover what you're passionate about and you choose the tools you want to practice your trade with, find a way to bring them all together

[to] create a message that isn't about selling something, but solving a problem."

Crean has been in business now for nearly two decades, so his start-up problems are now just memories. For Kristina Guerrero of Turbopup, a company that produces high-energy meal replacement bars for dogs, the growing pains are still fresh.

Guerrero is a former decorated Air Force pilot. During deployments in Afghanistan, Iraq, and at the Horn of Africa she earned two Combat Air Medals. When she started Turbopup, she got some assistance from the Women Veteran Entrepreneur Corps, a business growth initiative whose purpose is to help vets grow their start-ups quickly. Most of their assistance came in the form of useful information. That was great, but Guerrero was looking for more. She thought she'd found it in an invitation to appear on TV's *Shark Tank*.

We tend to think that any entrepreneur who goes on *Shark Tank* must be on the verge of success. Even though Guerrero's company had only $17,000 in sales in its first two years, she felt ready for the challenges posed by her TV appearance. She succeeded, receiving a $100,000 offer from Daymond John. When the show aired, her sales spiked dramatically, yet despite nearly a million in revenues, the company struggled to show a profit.

When Guerrero analyzed her predicament, she identified three concerns: trade shows, mass production costs, and some surprising setbacks that she should have prepared for. Guerrero learned the perils of trade shows when she attended some that were far away. She went to those shows because they were the biggest ones, but that was her mistake. Her company was too small, and her production potential wasn't great enough to supply the demands of big retail chains. "I should have stayed really local and done some trade shows that cost a lot less money," she now says. She advises those with start-ups to identify the most appropriate markets for their product and stay away from big ones until they have the kind of sustained increase in sales that will justify the entry fees for these larger venues. Not only are the big shows more expensive, but the larger retailers don't really want small-scale products that haven't yet been tested on a wider audience.

In her expansion, Guerrero had stopped making her dog treats in her kitchen and shifted production to a more dedicated facility. This took over a year and wound up requiring nine different trials before they got it right. The treat sizes, shapes, and baking methods were precise, and it took all those trials before she found a new facility that could do it right.

All entrepreneurs have to guard against surprise setbacks, and Turbopup was no exception. Guerrero's biggest hurdle appeared two months after she had completed a licensing agreement with a big pet products manufacturer. That's when TurboPup ran into an obstacle Guerrero could not have anticipated: America's worst bird flu outbreak in three decades.

Egg yolks, which are one of TurboPup's key ingredients, suddenly doubled in price.

Guerrero later told an interviewer: "As an entrepreneur, there are certain things that you expect to go wrong, [but] the devastating bird flu is not one of them." This was when her military experience helped her keep her head.

At this writing, in 2019, Turbopup seems to have overcome these obstacles. Dog owners can find Guerrero's treats in over a thousand PetSmart stores, and in other outlets throughout North America. Guerrero is philosophical about her entrepreneurial history. "As a veteran, nothing ever seems hard compared to what we've already been through," she says. "I've been shot at in combat!"

These former soldiers we've looked at in this chapter, and many others we've seen in earlier chapters, are great examples of the clear-eyed confidence and total competence our veterans bring to their entrepreneurial efforts. Their abilities and passionate commitment combine to put them among America's Best Business Owners.

Malcolm Allen

Veterans in Crisis: When the Going Gets Tough...

On December 22, 2018, the government of the United States officially shut down. This was nothing new. In the previous forty-two years, the government had come to a partial halt an average of every other year. What was different this time only became clear in the weeks that followed. No shutdown had ever lasted more than twenty-one days. That had been the one that started at the end of 1995 and lasted into the first week of 1996. It suspended services and paychecks and disrupted the daily life of millions of citizens.

The one that began in December 2018 would last five weeks. In the course of it, more than eight hundred thousand federal workers were idled, with their paychecks put on hold. With a workforce that's about one-third vets, that meant over a quarter of a million former soldiers were temporarily laid off from their jobs. Federal officials said most of these workers would receive those lost paychecks when the government opened, but as the weeks went by those promises lost their meaning. These suddenly unemployed workers had bills that would not wait.

One veteran of Operation Desert Storm in Iraq, Edward Canales, is the president of his local branch of the American Federation of Government Employees. Canales worked in federal prisons for twenty-six years, serving as a special investigative service technician. Though he recently retired, he still acts as a liaison officer for those veterans who are employed by the Federal Bureau of Prisons west of the Mississippi.

When the shutdown was barely a week old, calls flooded his union office from vets who were facing foreclosure, eviction, or bankruptcy if their next checks didn't come. As the shutdown continued, these calls took on a darker tone. Canales told ABC News that the vets had "no positive outlook on the future." He went on to sound this alarm: "If this shutdown does not stop, we are going to have fatalities. We're going to have suicides." Concerned that some of these veterans might injure themselves, or worse, Canales began referring the most worrisome calls to the Department of Veterans Affairs suicide hotline. Meanwhile, he learned that his own retirement checks were suspended for the duration of the shutdown.

As the shutdown entered its third week, several of the nation's largest and most influential veterans' groups joined together to speak out with one voice. These were the organizations known as the Big Six: The American Legion, Veterans of Foreign Wars, Vietnam Veterans of America, Paralyzed Veterans of

America, American Veterans, and Disabled American Veterans. Together these organizations have nearly five million members, which usually translates into the power to get things done in Washington.

Another veteran group, the Union Veterans Council, had already issued a statement earlier that week. "This shutdown has consequences that go beyond the loss of pay," the statement said. "These hard-working men and women who sacrificed so much for their country should not have their families held hostage by lawmakers that cannot relate to living paycheck to paycheck." Regis Riley, the national commander of American Veterans (AMVETS), one of the Big Six, added: "We ask the president and the Congress to get together, and get this situation resolved."

As the groups presented their statement, Veterans of Foreign Wars national commander, Vincent Lawrence, cited one veteran who had sought help from his organization. She was a single mother of three who had been put on leave without pay. Lacking a paycheck, she couldn't cover her rent or childcare. "She had approached a landlord and asked for some consideration during the partial government shutdown," Lawrence told reporters. "[S]he was denied that consideration, so she was reaching out to family members."

Before the shutdown began, Congress had already provided most of the funding for the Defense Department so active duty members of the Army, Navy, Marines, and Air Force still received their paychecks throughout the shutdown, but one military branch took a huge hit: The Coast Guard. This often-forgotten service that defends America's shores is a part of the Department of Homeland Security. This resulted in a situation where Coast Guard service members did not receive their paychecks but were still expected to come to work each day. They did.

The largest of the Big Six, The American Legion, came up with $1,500 grants for Coast Guard members who couldn't get by without them, but these funds could only go so far before they would run dry. "As a nonprofit, The American Legion is not capable of funding the entire Coast Guard payroll," said Brett Reistad, the Legion's National Commander.

As the shutdown dragged on, many vets now working for the government began to sink into despair. Toby Hauck is a six-year Air Force veteran who now works as an air traffic controller in Aurora, Illinois. He's also a representative for the National Air Traffic Controllers Association. Hauck's father and grandfather served in the U.S. military, and as the shutdown started, his son and daughter-in-law were about to begin a ten-month deployment overseas. Hauck and his wife, Lori, an intensive care nurse, planned to look after their toddler granddaughter until her parents come home. With both Toby and Lori working stressful jobs, the lack of federal paychecks only added to the burden.

"We show our pride every single day," Hauck told his interviewer. "When you talk on the frequency it's what runs through your blood. We love it, and we enjoy it." He paused, then explained: "We are hardworking, proud American employees doing a job for the American public that is essential . . . [Veterans] are very proud of our heritage and what we've done for the country. And those of us who continue to serve the federal government as federal employees continue that pride throughout [our] careers."

Hauck seemed disgusted, but Army veteran Tressa Rivera described her emotional reaction to the shutdown as "brokenhearted, upset, angry and sad." Rivera had recently moved from Georgia to Washington D.C. to take a job as a senior administrator with the Federal Emergency Management Agency (FEMA). She took a pay cut to do this because the job came with opportunities for advancement. With a daughter finishing high school and aiming at higher education, Rivera felt she needed those options. The shutdown threatened all her hopes and dreams.

As her furlough lengthened, Rivera told an interviewer: "I'm starting to feel it. As a vet, I also have PTSD. My anxiety has gone up. I don't sleep. I don't have an appetite. I'm scared of anything that looks like a potential bill." While sitting at home, her frustrations mounted as she read that many of her fellow Americans seemed unconcerned. Once they heard that the workers would eventually be paid, they assumed that there wasn't a problem. These people weren't factoring in fees, late payments, mortgages, and bills that needed to be paid, shutdown or not.

"I care about whether or not I can take my kid on her college visits," she told her interviewer. "I care whether or not I can go to the grocery store. I care whether my account is going to be overdrawn by the time all my bills come out in bill pay . . . These are the little things that people don't factor in when they say, 'Oh, well, you guys will get back pay.' Yeah, I don't really care about back pay right now. I care about whether or not I can get my insulin because I'm a Type 2 diabetic."

As she returned to work, Rivera was rethinking her options. She wondered if she could find work where she could be more creative, and perhaps even a job or a business that would allow her to work from home. The shutdown had left her disappointed, and even a little bitter. "I've given so much of my life to this country," she said, "and when I needed them to reciprocate, they didn't."

* * *

While many veterans were hurt by the shutdown, one former Marine gave some ex-soldiers a ray of hope. Iraq War Veteran, Nick Baucom, founder and CEO of Two Marines Moving, pledged to hire government employees idled by the shutdown, with an emphasis on workers who were also veterans. Two

Marines did this in both of its locations: Washington D.C. and Miami.

For over ten years, two Marines had been hiring veterans and even service members who were still on active duty. The moving business is seasonal, so the company always needs workers who are willing to adjust to flexible work schedules. This often fits well with vets who have recently separated. To them, the flexibility is a bonus. So is the fact that the company doesn't expect anyone to work there forever. It's transitional employment, and veterans who work there appreciate the company's vet-friendly culture.

Baucom inaugurated his hiring policy in the face of a temporarily shrinking market. During the shutdown, the company had suffered a 10% decrease in client move requests in Metro D.C. Despite all that, Baucom remained committed to his policy. "This isn't the company's first time going through a government shutdown," he told reporters.

Our nation's soldiers and ex-soldiers are committed to their country, and this commitment runs parallel with their loyalty to one another. As a former Marine, Baucom knows this, and he practices it in his business. When his fellow vets need him, he's there.

There are countless vets like Baucom all over the country who share that commitment. Some have their own businesses, while others work because they want that regular paycheck. These are the people who've protected us, allowing us to go about our daily business without fear of foreign attack. Many of them relish the competition of the business world, but, like Baucom, they share a keen understanding of their responsibilities to their communities. When they hire workers, they are always on the lookout for veterans, and they also give many young people their first work experience.

These veteran entrepreneurs aren't just good businesspeople; they are also among the best citizens our country has. They understand that when trouble is on the horizon, they share in the responsibility for dealing with it. Trouble is what they've been trained for. They meet it with determination, competence, and endurance.

When Nick Baucom announced his hiring policy, he gave this simple explanation of his motivation: "Although I may no longer be on active duty, my company and I continue to serve our country every day."

About the Author

Malcolm Allen is a recognized expert on human potential and (BCSA) Board Certified Social Advocate. He migrates effortlessly between corporate boardrooms and underserved communities aiming to advance the interests of social justice, particularly on behalf of populations or groups who have been disadvantaged, disempowered, or forgotten.

Allen has authored over two dozen books, and most have achieved best-selling status. He has worked with subject matter experts and credentialed instruction designers to socially engineer a platform of outcome-based programs that provide solutions for disabled veterans, recidivism, human trafficking, dropout prevention, bullying, diversity, mentoring, financial inclusion, entrepreneurship, and leadership. All programs are Military Approved, and available at Penn Foster College and Graduate America Centers of Excellence around the world. For seminar licensing, book purchases, or speaker requests, please visit: Unconditional.org

www.ingramcontent.com/pod-product-compliance
Lightning Source LLC
Chambersburg PA
CBHW031055180526
45163CB00002BA/847